The Thirteen Colonies

North Carolina

Books in the Thirteen Colonies series include:

Delaware
Georgia
Maryland
Massachusetts
New Hampshire
New Jersey
New York
North Carolina
Pennsylvania
Rhode Island
South Carolina
Virginia
The Thirteen Colonies: Primary Sources

12/02
$22

The Thirteen Colonies

North Carolina

Michael V. Uschan

Lucent Books, Inc.
P.O. Box 289011, San Diego, California

To Carol Uschan: Hope you enjoy the book!

On cover: Carolina family in log cabin home

Library of Congress Cataloging-in-Publication Data

Uschan, Michael V., 1948–
    North Carolina / by Michael V. Uschan.
        p. cm. — (The thirteen colonies)
    Includes bibliographical references and index.
    ISBN 1-56006-885-X (alk. paper)
        1. North Carolina—History—Colonial period, ca. 1600–1775—
    Juvenile literature. 2. North Carolina—History—1775-1865—Juvenile
    literature. [1. North Carolina—History—Colonial period, ca. 1600–1776.
    2. North Carolina—History—1775–1865.] I. Title. II. Thirteen colonies
    (Lucent books)
    F257 .U8 2001
    975.6'02—dc21

Printed in the U.S.A.

Contents

Foreword
6

Introduction • North Carolina: A Colony of
Bewitching Beauty and Danger
8

Chapter One • North Carolina's Difficult Beginning
13

Chapter Two • The Colony Struggles to Grow
29

Chapter Three • Life in Colonial North Carolina
48

Chapter Four • North Carolina in the Revolutionary War
64

Chapter Five • North Carolina: Learning to Live in Freedom
80

Notes 96

Chronology 100

For Further Reading 103

Works Consulted 104

Index 106

Picture Credits 112

About the Author 112

Foreword

T he story of the thirteen English colonies that became the United States of America is one of startling diversity, conflict, and cultural evolution. Today, it is easy to assume that the colonists were of one mind when fighting for independence from England and afterwards when the national government was created. However, the American colonies had to overcome a vast reservoir of distrust rooted in the broad geographical, economic, and social differences that separated them. Even the size of the colonies contributed to the conflict; the smaller states feared domination by the larger ones.

These sectional differences stemmed from the colonies' earliest days. The northern colonies were more populous and their economies were more diverse, being based on both agriculture and manufacturing. The southern colonies, however, were dependent on agriculture—in most cases, the export of only one or two staple crops. These economic differences led to disagreements over things such as the trade embargo the Continental Congress imposed against England during the war. The southern colonies wanted their staple crops to be exempt from the embargo because their economies would have collapsed if they could not trade with England, which in some cases was the sole importer. A compromise was eventually made and the southern colonies were allowed to keep trading some exports.

In addition to clashing over economic issues, often the colonies did not see eye to eye on basic political philosophy. For example, Connecticut leaders held that education was the route to greater political liberty, believing that knowledgeable citizens would not allow themselves to be stripped of basic freedoms and rights. South Carolinians, on the other hand, thought that the protection of personal property and economic independence was the basic foundation of freedom. In light of such profound differences it is amazing that the colonies were able to unite in the fight for independence and then later under a strong national government.

Why, then, did the colonies unite? When the Revolutionary War began the colonies set aside their differences and banded together because they shared a common goal—gaining political freedom from what they considered a tyrannical monarchy—that could be more easily attained if they cooperated with each other. However, after the war ended, the states abandoned unity and once again pursued sectional interests, functioning as little nations in a weak confederacy. The congress of this confederacy, which was bound by the Articles of Confederation, had virtually no authority over the individual states. Much bickering ensued—the individual states refused to pay their war debts to the national government, the nation was sinking further into an economic depression, and there was nothing the national government could do. Political leaders realized that the nation was in jeopardy of falling apart. They were also aware that European nations such as England, France, and Spain were all watching the new country, ready to conquer it at the first opportunity. Thus the states came together at the Constitutional Convention in order to create a system of government that would be both strong enough to protect them from invasion and yet nonthreatening to state interests and individual liberties.

The Thirteen Colonies series affords the reader a thorough understanding of how the development of the individual colonies helped create the United States. The series examines the early history of each colony's geographical region, the founding and first years of each colony, daily life in the colonies, and each colony's role in the American Revolution. Emphasis is given to the political, economic, and social uniqueness of each colony. Both primary and secondary quotes enliven the text, and sidebars highlight personalities, legends, and personal stories. Each volume ends with a chapter on how the colony dealt with changes after the war and its role in developing the U.S. Constitution and the new nation. Together, the books in this series convey a remarkable story—how thirteen fiercely independent colonies came together in an unprecedented political experiment that not only succeeded, but endures to this day.

Introduction

North Carolina: A Colony of Bewitching Beauty and Danger

The first European explorers and settlers who saw North Carolina fell in love with it because of its great physical beauty, which varies dramatically from the wave-washed seacoast to the towering heights of the Blue Ridge Mountains, and its abundant natural resources, which promised a rich life for those who would work hard to tame this strange new land. The hold the area exerted on these early visitors is indicated by the glowing reports they sent back to Europe.

In March 1524 Italian mariner Giovanni da Verrazano sailed his ship *La Dauphine* along the North Carolina coast from Cape Fear north to present-day Kitty Hawk. Naming the area Arcadia, Verrazano penned the earliest description of the area in a dispatch to King Francis I of France, who had financed his expedition. Published in 1582 in Richard Hakluyt's *Divers Voyages Touching the Discoverie of America and the Islands Adjacent,* Verrazano's tribute helped influence the English to choose North Carolina as the location of their first attempt to colonize the New World. The explorer described a land of "faire fields and plains" with "good and wholesome aire," trees "greater and better than any in Europe," and "sweet and odoriferous flowers," an area that was, all in all, "as pleasant and delectable to behold, as is possible to imagine."[1]

In 1650 Englishman Edward Williams described the emerging British colony as "a country whom God and Nature has indulged with blessings [unknown] to any other region,"[2] and in 1709 John Lawson, in his *History of Carolina,* claimed, "The Inhabitants of Carolina, through the richness of the soil, live an easy and pleasant life."[3] One colonist who arrived in 1711 lauded his new home to friends back in England:

> This country is praised too lightly in Europe and condemned too much. I hope also in a few years to have cows and swine as much as I desire. Of vermin, snakes, and such like, there is not so much as they tell of in Europe. I have seen crocodiles [alligators] by the water but they soon fled. Stags and deer, ducks and geese and turkeys are numerous.[4]

But this newcomer also understood that his bold move to the New World was not without risk. "The land is good," he admitted, "but the beginning is hard, the journey dangerous."[5]

Italian explorer Giovanni da Verrazano wrote the earliest description of what is today North Carolina.

Danger Mixed with Beauty

North Carolina's beauty and natural riches blinded colonists to the hardships they would encounter in a land unlike any they had ever known. By the seventeenth century, Europe had been settled for hundreds of years and had no wilderness left to tame. Because the English were unfamiliar with such vast uninhabited spaces, they could not imagine the dangers they would face. By the late 1580s, the two earliest attempts to establish an English presence in the New World on North Carolina's Roanoke Island would both fail, with the latter producing the legend of the "Lost Colony," a mystery that baffles historians to this very day: How could more than a hundred men, women, and children have disappeared?

An English governor returns to Roanoke Island from England to find the colony deserted. The mysterious disappearance of the colonists created the legend of the "Lost Colony."

The first settlers who began moving into North Carolina around 1650 had to deal with a wide variety of perils and problems in the early decades of the colony's difficult, tenuous existence, from disease and a scarcity of food and supplies to raids along the seacoast by pirates. But of all the dangers, the greatest was the constant threat of war from the people who had lived there for thousands of years.

When the first European settlers stepped ashore on Roanoke, between thirty thousand and thirty-five thousand Indians belonging to about thirty tribes inhabited what would become one of the original thirteen colonies. The arrival of the newcomers would prove tragic for the land's original occupants, who had lived in modern-day North Carolina for over ten thousand years. In *North Carolina: The History of a Southern State,* Hugh Talmadge Lefler and Albert Ray Newsome explain that war between Indians and colonists was unavoidable:

> At first, relations between the two races in North Carolina were relatively peaceful, though there were occasional minor conflicts. But the aggressive, if not contemptuous attitude of the whites and the resentment of the natives, together with conflicting and irreconcilable interests, made hostilities inevitable. The Indians faced the problem of survival, both as a people and as individuals.[6]

Within a century, North Carolina's Native Americans would lose their land and their freedom. And it was the colonists' desire for their own freedom that would lead to war with England, the colony's mother country.

Unruly British Subjects

Until the Revolutionary War, North Carolina was ruled by either the lords proprietors, eight members of royalty who in 1663 were granted ownership of the colony, or the king of England, who in 1729 took it back because of the ineffective way the proprietors governed the colony. But historian William B. Hesseltine explains that no matter who ruled them, North Carolina settlers could be rebellious:

Politically, the history of North Carolina from its settlement to the outbreak of the Revolution is a long story of conflict between the people and [their British rulers]. For the most part, the ruling officials were the opponents of the turbulent frontier democracy which developed in the colony.[7]

North Carolinians were unruly subjects because they wanted the freedom to govern themselves; they fought for their rights, protested laws they believed were unfair, and forced some governors out of office. Only a little more than a century after North Carolina became a colony, its residents were among the first to declare their independence from Great Britain, and their state was the scene of several battles that helped Americans win the Revolution.

Chapter One

North Carolina's Difficult Beginning

Although North Carolina is often called a "state without a birthday"[8] because there is no record of when the first permanent European settlers arrived, documents do exist on the first attempt to create a colony there. In July 1526 Spanish explorer Lucas Vázquez de Ayllón traveled from Santo Domingo, a Spanish possession in the Caribbean, to establish a stronghold at the mouth of the Cape Fear River. He was accompanied by more than five hundred men and women, including what are believed to be the first African American slaves to set foot in what would one day become the United States.

De Ayllón's attempt at colonization, however, began and ended in disaster. As the expedition entered the Cape Fear River, one of its two ships was wrecked and valuable supplies were lost, and for the next few months the Spanish suffered from starvation and illness. Finally on October 18, with de Ayllón among those who had died and their number reduced to about 150, the remnants of the would-be colony fled on foot to Spanish outposts to the south.

North Carolina's Unusual Geography

The geography of all thirteen original colonies played a role in their development and early history, but none more so than that of North Carolina, whose unique topography slowed its early growth and influences its fortunes even today. In North Carolina: The History of a Southern State, *Hugh Talmadge Lefler and Albert Ray Newsome comment on the state's unique physical characteristics:*

North Carolina is divided into three rather clearly defined geographic areas: the Coastal Plain, the Piedmont Plateau, and the Mountains. Almost two-fifths of the state's area lies within the Coastal Plain [which extends westward from the Atlantic Ocean] a distance varying from 100 to 150 miles. Along the coast for a distance of some 175 miles there is a long chain of islands, or banks, ranging in height from a few feet to that of Kill Devil Hill in Dare County, which is more than a hundred feet high. From these sandbanks along the coast, three capes with awe-inspiring names jut out into the ocean; Hatteras, extending into the Graveyard of the Atlantic, Lookout, and Cape Fear. Between the banks and the mainland proper are two large sounds, Pamlico and Albemarle, and several smaller ones. . . . The Piedmont Plateau embraces almost two-fifths of North Carolina's area. Almost from the start the region developed a diversified economy. Topography, soil, climate, forests, and other factors tended to retard the cultivation of large tracts of land and caused the Piedmont to develop as an area of small farms cultivated chiefly by white labor, and this led to the development of a more democratic social order than prevailed in the eastern portion of North Carolina. The third physical region of North Carolina embraces the mountains of the Southern Appalachians [extending from the irregular chain known as the Blue Ridge on the east to that long chain known as the Smoky Mountains on the west]. This beautiful region covers an area of about six thousand square miles. It contains forty-nine peaks over 6,000 feet and 175 of over 5,000.

Historian William S. Powell comments on the only traces ever found of the first Europeans who tried to settle North Carolina: "Their route of march down the coast from the Cape Fear was identified many years later by the bits of rusted armor and other equipment that marked the spots where the sick and dying had fallen by the wayside."[9]

Six decades after de Ayllón's disastrous attempt to settle North Carolina, the English tried to make it a colony. And although their first efforts would meet with failure, the vision that one man had for his country's future would eventually lead to North America becoming an English possession.

Sir Walter Raleigh

The story of English colonization of the New World began in June 1578 when Queen Elizabeth I gave Sir Humphrey Gilbert permission to settle a huge area in North America that included North Carolina. When Gilbert died before he could act on the generous gift, the queen renewed the grant on March 25, 1584, in the name of Sir Walter Raleigh, his half-brother. Although Raleigh never set foot in the New World, this English lord did more than any single person to spark English settlement there. In *A History of the American People,* Paul Johnson notes that Raleigh, who had already been successful as a military leader and government official, had many of the attributes that would distinguish the people who would eventually populate the vast new land he wanted to colonize:

Raleigh was, in a sense, a proto-American. He had certain strongly marked characteristics which were to be associated with the American archetype. He was energetic, brash, hugely ambitious, money-conscious . . . far-sighted and ahead of his time, with a passion for the new and, not least, a streak of idealism, which clashed violently with his desire to make a fortune.[10]

This farsighted Englishman believed his country needed to colonize an unknown new land thousands of miles across the Atlantic

Sir Walter Raleigh convinced the English government to colonize the New World in order to compete with Spain.

Ocean because Spain, an enemy England battled around the world, was already growing rich and powerful from its New World holdings. Raleigh knew that if England did not create its own colonies, Spain would grow powerful enough to conquer his homeland.

Roanoke Island

After receiving permission from Queen Elizabeth to explore the New World, Raleigh in the spring of 1584 dispatched an expedition led by Captains Philip Amadas and Arthur Barlowe to locate a suitable site for a colony. The explorers landed on the North Carolina coast on July 13, claimed it for England, and settled on Roanoke Island, known as the birthplace of English America. Roanoke is part of North Carolina's Outer Banks, a thin line of islands, banks, and sandbars that stretch 175 miles along its coast.

After scouting Roanoke and the mainland, the party sailed home with detailed, glowing comments about this rich new land. Barlowe poetically enumerated the many virtues of what he called "the goodliest land under the cope of heaven," which had soil that was

England's Queen Elizabeth gave Sir Walter Raleigh permission to explore the New World in search of a suitable site for a colony.

"sweet, fruitfull and wholesome," cedar trees that were the "highest and reddest in the world," and waters filled with "the goodliest and best fish."[11] The reports by Barlowe and other early chroniclers were overly generous in their praise because they were trying to excite Europeans about colonizing the New World.

Queen Elizabeth was thrilled with the prospect of establishing an English possession that could enrich her kingdom. On January 6, 1585, she knighted Raleigh and gave him permission to name the land Virginia in honor of herself. (Elizabeth, who ruled Great Britain from 1558 to 1603, was called the Virgin Queen because she never married.) The original colony named Virginia was a vast land that extended as far south as Spanish possessions in Florida and included the modern-day states of Virginia, North Carolina, South Carolina, and Tennessee.

The Ralph Lane Colony

In April 1585 Raleigh dispatched a large force of several hundred men commanded by his cousin, Sir Richard Grenville, to establish a colony on Roanoke Island. Most members of this group were English, but some were from Ireland, Wales, Germany, and Holland, and their ranks included John White, an artist, and Thomas Harriot, an Oxford professor. After returning home, White painted the first pictures of English colonists in America and Harriot wrote a book that provided the first detailed account of the New World.

Ralph Lane was governor of the expedition, which arrived at Roanoke on July 21 and immediately began building Fort Raleigh on the island's north end. Lane also wrote the first letter from the New World. It was delivered by Grenville, who returned to England in August to report on progress being made in establishing a colony. In the letter Lane, who stayed behind with 107 others, praised Roanoke Island and the coastal areas he and his men had explored:

> It is the goodliest and most pleasing territorie of the world
> ... and the climate so wholesome, that we have had not one
> sick, since we touched land here. To conclude, if Virginia had
> but Horses and Kine [cattle] in some reasonable proportion
> ... no realme in Christendom were comparable to it.[12]

Lane exaggerated the New World's riches while failing to mention problems he and his party encountered in their attempt at creating a colony. For one thing, Lane had clashed continuously with Grenville over how to organize and run the fledgling colony. Another obstacle to the colony's success was that Lane's men were not very interested in tilling the soil, building houses, and doing other hard work

In *A Brief and True Report of the New Found Land of Virginia*, Thomas Harriot criticized Ralph Lane's men for not having the spirit of true settlers.

necessary to establish a permanent home. In his 1588 book *A Brief and True Report of the New Found Land of Virginia,* Harriot criticized Lane's men for not having the spirit of true settlers, claiming they spent most of their time searching for treasure: "After gold and silver was not to be found, as it was by them looked for, they had little or no care for any other thing but to pamper their bellies."[13] They were mostly soldiers, so it is not strange that they were uninterested in the drudgery of establishing a colony.

Living conditions gradually worsened because Grenville failed to return with food and supplies. When noted explorer Sir Francis Drake arrived on June 10, 1586, to check on the colonists after battling the Spanish in the Caribbean, Lane decided everyone should sail back to England with him. Ironically, Grenville finally returned with the needed supplies just a few days later. Finding the colony abandoned, Grenville left a small contingent of fifteen men and headed home himself.

Lane's colony failed, but it was historically significant as the first attempt to establish an English presence in the New World. The reports Lane and his men brought back of the new land also helped spur future efforts to settle there.

The Lost Colony

Raleigh was still determined to create a British colony, and by the spring of 1587 he had enlisted the financial backing of more than thirty merchants and other wealthy men for another attempt. Raleigh named John White governor of this second group of 120 settlers, which included seventeen women and nine children and left England on May 8. When they arrived at Roanoke Island on July 22, there was no trace of the fifteen men Lane had left behind except for a few bones scattered about. This suggested that they had been killed, either by Indians or Spanish soldiers who sometimes visited the area.

Despite the fear engendered by the absence of Lane's men, the colonists began to clean up Fort Raleigh and the houses Lane's men had built. The second attempt to establish a colony went well at first, and an important event occurred on August 18, 1587, when a girl was born to Ananias and Eleanor Dare. White, who was Eleanor's

Virginia Dare, the first English child born in the New World, is baptized into Christianity.

father, wrote in his journal that the baby was named Virginia "because this childe was the first Christian born in Virginia [and the New World]."[14] On August 27, White sailed back to England to get more supplies and colonists.

White returned home to find his country at war with Spain, and Queen Elizabeth soon ordered that every ship was needed to defend England. Unable to secure a ship for several years, White did not return to the colony until August 17, 1590, the day before his granddaughter's third birthday. White wrote that after his ship had reached Roanoke Island at nightfall, he and members of the crew vainly tried to make contact with the colonists: "We let fall our [anchor] neere the shore, and sounded with a trumpet a Call, and afterwardes many familiar English tunes and songs, and called to them friendly; but we had no answere."[15]

There was no response because there was no one to hear their cries. The next day when White and his men inspected Fort Raleigh, they discovered no trace of life and almost everything that could have been carried away was gone. The only clues to the disappearance of the colonists were the words CRO and CROATOAN, which had been carved into trees. White wrote, "One of the chiefe trees at the right side of the entrance [to the fort] had the barke taken off and 5. foote from the ground in fayre Capitall letters was graven CROATOAN without any crosse or signe of distresse."[16]

White had told the colonists that if they had to flee because of danger, they should put a Maltese cross next to any message they left. But there was no cross next to the carved letters, which added to the mystery of what happened. If there had not been any trouble, why had the colonists left the safety of the fort and the other buildings, which had not been destroyed?

A Historical Mystery

Croatoan, the area now known as Hatteras, was the home of Manteo, an Indian friendly to the colonists, and the message indicated colonists might have gone there. However, after a violent storm damaged his ships, White had to discontinue his search for members of what became known as the Lost Colony and was forced to return to England. In *Roanoke Island: The Beginnings of*

When Governor John White returned to Roanoke Island in 1590, he found the colony deserted. The words CRO and CROATOAN carved into trees served as the only clues to the colonists' disappearance.

English America, historian David Stick summarizes the basic theories about what happened to the Lost Colony:

> Did the colonists, as White surmised, leave Roanoke Island to take up permanent residence with the Croatoan Indians near Cape Hatteras? If so, are their descendants still living? Or did they move farther into the interior [and join another tribe]? Some have contended that they were wiped out by disease—or by famine. Others advance the theory that they attempted to return to England in one of the small vessels left them by White, only to disappear in the vastness of the Atlantic. Still others are convinced that they were attacked and killed by Wanchese [a Native American] and the Roanoakes, or by the Indians of Powhatan's Jamestown-area confederacy, or by the Spaniards. What happened to the Lost Colony? No one really knows—and very likely no one ever will. The fate of Raleigh's colonists remains as much a mystery as before.[17]

The most commonly accepted explanation is that Indians killed the colonists. The revealing part about that theory is how quickly relations between colonists and Native Americans changed from friendship to open warfare.

The Original Americans

Verrazano in 1524 had been the first European to make contact with Native Americans in what was to become North Carolina. In his report, the Italian explorer said the Indians he and his crew encountered were "charmed by their first sight of white men,"[18] and that when a sailor who was tossing them mirrors, bells, and other small gifts accidentally fell overboard, the Indians took him ashore and helped him dry his clothes over a fire. The Indians, Verrazano wrote, were "very courteous and friendly," and when the sailor returned to the boat, they accompanied him "with great love, clapping him fast about with many embracings."[19]

Sixty years later, Amadas and Barlowe encountered Native Americans on their third day on Roanoke Island. It was from them that the two Englishmen learned the island's name, and when the explorers returned to England, they took along two of the friendliest Indians, Wanchese and Manteo. The duo became popular in England, helping to excite interest in the New World.

Wanchese and Manteo were members of the Croatoan, a tribe later known as the Lumbee. Each of the thirty tribes then living in North Carolina spoke a different language, all of which were from

A Debt Owed to Native Americans

Although their relationship with English colonists would soon turn bitter, Native Americans were at first helpful to the newcomers to their land. In North Carolina: A Bicentennial History, *William S. Powell explains how Indians helped the colonists who tried to settle Roanoke Island in 1585:*

Indians proved to be good sources of information for the colonists, as many of the Englishmen were good students of Indian culture. From the natives [Ralph] Lane's men learned to make dugout canoes. They also learned to plant crops in rows and hills, as well as to keep weeds out of their gardens. This was a particularly important lesson for them. In England, where land had been tilled for generations, a field would be plowed and the seed [spread] over it. In America, however, the warm climate and the presence of weed seeds would not permit this. Such a field would quickly be covered with vigorous weeds of many kinds. They also adopted the Indians' name for unfamiliar things, hence *moccasin, canoe, hickory, persimmon, opossum, raccoon, tomahawk, hurricane, hominy,* and a host of other Indian words began to enter the English language.

Other Native Americans were also friendly to settlers, most notably in Jamestown, Virginia, and Plymouth, Massachusetts. In The United States to 1865, *Michael Kraus explains that Indians helped them survive:*

"When the earliest settlers faced starvation, hospitable Indians brought them fish and maize [corn]. The Plymouth colony and the Jamestown settlement were rescued from disaster by supplies from either the Algonquian, Iroquoian, or Siouan linguistic families. The most important tribes were the Cherokee of the western mountains, the only one that still has a presence today in its native land; the Hatteras, who lived along the coast; and the Tuscarora, whose territory extended inward from the sea.

From the start, the English looked down on Native Americans because they were culturally different. Harriot wrote, "In respect to

the natives, who not only brought them food but taught them how to grow Indian corn, which matured rapidly."

Although the relationship between English colonists and Native Americans rapidly deteriorated, the English initially learned many valuable lessons in farming and survival from the natives.

Native Americans feasting and celebrating in the village of Secota in North Carolina.

us, they are a people poore, and for want of skil and judgement in the knowledge and use of our things, doe esteeme our trifles before things of greater value."[20] For their part, the Indians quickly came to consider the colonists intruders who wanted to steal their land, and a series of incidents created bitter feelings on both sides. For example, after an Indian stole a silver cup, the Lane colonists killed him and burned an Indian village near Lake Mattamuskeet. Historian David B. Quinn writes that it took only a few months for Indians to turn against Lane's men: "The settlers had been acceptable as temporary god-like visitors in 1585; in 1586 they had become men who threatened the security of Indian society and aroused savage cupidity [greed] by their wealth."[21]

In May 1586 Lane's men fought with the Secotan tribe, which lived on Roanoke Island, and in the battle they killed Wingina, the Secotan's chief. Although not all Native Americans were hostile to the Lane and White colonies, future relations between Indians and colonists throughout America would mirror those first few encounters in the 1580s—the two sides would almost always quickly learn to hate each other and conflict would be inevitable. The hostility of Native Americans was a key factor in destroying Raleigh's dream of establishing an English presence in North Carolina.

Jamestown: The First Colony

Despite his failure to establish a colony on Roanoke Island, Raleigh's efforts were important because they stimulated interest in colonizing the New World. Raleigh himself always believed his nation would one day accomplish what he could not: "I shall yet live to see it an English nation."[22]

That day finally came in 1606, when a group of wealthy men created the Virginia Company of London after King James I, Queen Elizabeth's successor to the English throne, authorized them to establish a New World colony. The Virginia Company dispatched three ships bearing 105 men, and they arrived at Chesapeake Bay in April 1607. The party sailed thirty miles up the Powhatan River, which they renamed the James after their king, and located the first permanent English colony on a peninsula. They honored their king once again by naming the settlement Jamestown. This first successful British colony was less than fifty miles north of today's North Carolina border. It was from this first tiny English foothold in the New World that the people who became known as Americans would travel across and populate an entire continent.

Jamestown, however, struggled to grow in its early years because of a variety of problems, including disease, conflicts with Native Americans, and poor harvests that left people near starvation; by the 1620s only two thousand colonists remained alive of the more than ten thousand that had been sent to Virginia. In 1624 King James I was so unhappy with the way the Virginia Company had governed the colony that he revoked its charter and made it a royal colony, one directly under his direction.

Carolana

Virginia, however, did not remain in the king's possession for long. In 1629 Charles I, the new English king, gave the southern half of Virginia to Sir Robert Heath, his attorney general. In honor of the king, the area was named Carolana, Latin for Charles, but it soon became known as Carolina. The new colony extended south from Virginia to what is now the Georgia-Florida state line and all the way west to the "South Seas," the English name then for the Pacific Ocean.

When Heath failed to settle Carolina, title to the grant passed through several hands before March 24, 1663, when another king, Charles II, gave it to eight of his favorite nobles, powerful men who had helped him regain his throne after a civil war. By the time these eight lords proprietors received Carolina, however, the hardy pioneers who would settle it had already begun making their homes there.

Chapter Two

The Colony Struggles to Grow

N orth Carolina's most unique natural feature is its Outer Banks, a slender chain of islands and sandbars that form a barrier separating the Atlantic Ocean from the mainland. The Outer Banks were significant for providing the first site for an English colony in the New World, Roanoke Island. But historians Hugh Talmadge Lefler and Albert Ray Newsome claim that the difficulty the Outer Banks created for ships trying to reach the mainland, and the coast's lack of places for oceangoing ships to land, combined to slow the colony's early growth:

The treacherous coast and lack of good ports were major factors in diverting English colonization to the Chesapeake region after the failure of the [Sir Walter] Raleigh colonies at Roanoke Island. When permanent settlement of North Carolina began almost a century later, the absence of good harbors retarded colonization directly from Europe, and consequently the colony was settled largely "as an overflow

Colonists had begun settling in Carolina when Charles II granted the land to eight lords proprietors.

from other colonies," notably Virginia, South Carolina, and Pennsylvania.[23]

North Carolina's unusual coastal geography was one of three major obstacles to its early development. The other two factors were the many dangers that confronted settlers, including battles with Native Americans and attacks by pirates, and inept rule by the eight lords proprietors who had been granted Carolina by King Charles II. Despite problems that awaited them in the new colony, people came anyway for one main reason—the chance to own land.

Free Land

The first known white settler was Nathaniel Batts, a fur trader who built a home in the Albemarle Sound area in northeastern North Carolina about 1650. Gradually, more and more people arrived from Virginia and other colonies. These first North Carolinians endured many hardships to establish new homes, as an official report from the 1660s clearly indicates:

> It had pleased God in his Providence to inflict such a generall calamitie upon the inhabitants . . . that for Severall yeares they had nott injoyed the fruitts of their labours which causes them generally to growne [groan] under the burtyn [burden] of poverty and many times famine.[24]

Problems they faced included bad weather (hurricanes, heavy rains, and drought), natural predators that killed livestock, illness,

North Carolina settlers endured many hardships such as bad weather, predators that killed their livestock, and difficulty in obtaining supplies.

and difficulty in obtaining supplies. But historian Louis B. Wright explains that people were willing to endure such hardships because in Europe only royalty or the very rich could own property:

> The most impelling single motive was the desire for land and all that the possession of broad acres implied. Land hunger frequently was joined with other considerations—the lure of adventure, the desire for religious freedom, or any number of a multitude of frustrations at home—but the emigrant's brightest dream was the vision of [owning] land. Even the poorest servant, who sold himself into a four-year bondage to pay his passage, had a hope of ultimately settling upon a piece of ground which he would own.[25]

In order to attract new residents, the proprietors adopted the *headright* system, in which each *head* (colonist) who moved to North Carolina had the *right* to fifty acres of unoccupied land. Free land was available even to former indentured servants, men and women who had worked for several years as virtual slaves for other colonists to pay the price of their passage to America. The proprietors levied an annual tax, usually a half-penny an acre. It was called a *quitrent* because payment *quit*, or ended, any further obligation the colonists owed for that year to proprietors, the true owners of the land. The proprietors also granted or sold larger tracts of land, sometimes thousands of acres, to friends or business associates for plantations that grew tobacco and other crops.

Early Settlers

Despite the promise of free land, the fledgling colony grew slowly and by 1694 it still had only about four thousand residents. It did not get its first incorporated town, Bath, until March 8, 1706, but by 1710 settlements stretched from the Virginia border to the Albemarle Sound, most of them along the banks of the Roanoke, Pamlico, and Neuse Rivers. Most early communities started along rivers—Bath is on a bluff overlooking the Pamlico River—because waterways served the same purpose as highways do today: They

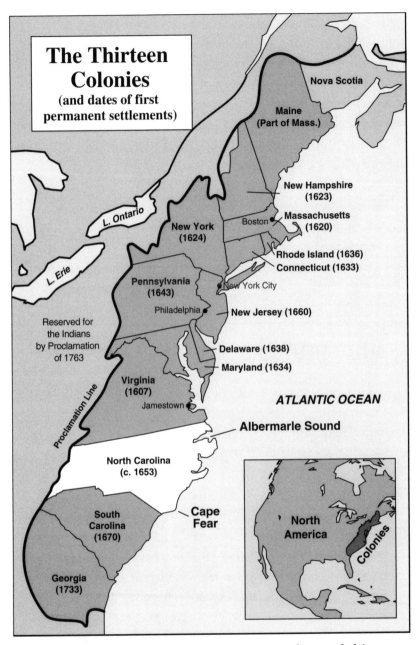

The Thirteen Colonies
(and dates of first permanent settlements)

Nova Scotia

Maine
(Part of Mass.)

New Hampshire
(1623)

L. Ontario

New York
(1624)

Boston

Massachusetts
(1620)

Rhode Island (1636)
Connecticut (1633)

L. Erie

Pennsylvania
(1643)

New York City

Philadelphia

New Jersey (1660)

Reserved for
the Indians
by Proclamation
of 1763

Delaware (1638)
Maryland (1634)

Virginia
(1607)

Jamestown

ATLANTIC OCEAN

Proclamation Line

Albermarle Sound

North Carolina
(c. 1653)

Cape
Fear

North
America

Colonies

South
Carolina
(1670)

Georgia
(1733)

made it easier for people to travel, receive supplies, and ship crops and products they wanted to sell.

Transplants from other colonies were joined by emigrants from Europe and the West Indies, another English possession. Among the new arrivals in 1705 were French Huguenots, who had been persecuted in Catholic France because they were Protestant. In 1710 immigrants from Switzerland and Germany bought 17,500 acres of land at the junction of the Trent and Neuse Rivers and founded New Bern. They were led by Baron Christoph von Graffenried, who named the town Neuse-Bern after his home city in Switzerland (Bern) and one of the rivers near the new community. English colonists thought the name sounded like New Bern, which is what the town came to be called. Graffenried helped design the community:

> Since in America they do not like to live crowded, in order to enjoy a purer air, I accordingly ordered the streets to be very broad and the houses well separated, one from the other. I marked three acres of land for each family, for house, barn, garden, orchard, hemp field, poultry yard and

Indentured Servants and Slaves

Tens of thousands of people who helped settle the New World arrived as indentured servants, members of a system of economic enslavement that temporarily took away their rights as free citizens. In the last two-thirds of the seventeenth century, 1,500 to 2,000 men, women, and children were transported annually to North Carolina, Virginia, and other southern English colonies as indentured servants. In A History of the South, *William B. Hesseltine explains that indentured servitude eased two problems—the need for cheap labor and the fact that many people could not afford to immigrate to New World colonies:*

> To solve the problem of bringing the labor force of England to the eager tobacco planters, the system of indentured servitude was devised. There were two classes of indentured servants, voluntary and involuntary. In the former class were numbered those English laborers who, in return for passage, entered into bonds of indenture with ship captains. Arriving in the colonies, the captains sold the indentures to planters of tobacco. In Virginia, the laborer could work out his passage in four or five years. At the end of that period he [women, as well, came to the colonies as indentured servants]

other purposes. I divided the village like a cross and in the middle I intended the church.[26]

Within a year, however, New Bern was destroyed. It was burned to the ground by Tuscarora Indians who resented the invasion of their home by four hundred settlers.

The Tuscarora War

New Bern had displaced a nearby Native American community called Chattoka. Colonists routinely stole land from Indians, enslaved them, and unintentionally introduced infectious diseases such as measles that killed thousands of them. These injustices led to minor uprisings by the Coree tribe in 1703 and the Meherrin in 1707, and the constant threat of Indian warfare scared away many settlers.

could be free in a country where land was cheap, wages high, and opportunities abundant.

As the need for cheap labor increased due to the establishment of big plantations, which required many workers for crops like tobacco, English colonists enslaved both Native Americans and Africans. A Dutch ship that arrived at Jamestown, Virginia, in 1619 with twenty captive African natives began African American slavery in America. In The Smithsonian Guides to Historic America: The Carolinas and the Appalachian States, *Patricia Hudson and Sandra L. Ballard explain slavery in North Carolina:*

Slavery was not unique to the South; it was merely more successful there, and inextricably associated with race. Black slavery united the seacoast, the highlands, and the plains beyond [North Carolina], and distinguished the frontier experience of the South from that of the North. The English applied their habit of using conquered people for slave labor as soon as they stepped ashore. Coffles [chained groups] of conquered Indians dragged themselves eastward through the dust toward the Carolina coast, and met there blacks who, a few months earlier, had been marched westward toward the holding pens on the coast of Africa.

Why Leave England?

People today still marvel why anyone would risk a dangerous ocean voyage of thousands of miles to travel to a wild new country where they would have to struggle just to survive. But in The Shaping of the American Past, *historian Robert Kelley explains that immigration to the New World was preferable to many people than remaining in England, where conditions for average people were dismal:*

There were about four million of them, living mainly in thousands of villages in the south of England, and they were hungry all the time. It was the year 1600, Elizabeth was still on the throne, and as usual, famine was a constant fear. In England's small cities and in great London with its 300,000 souls, food could normally be found, but practically everyone lived in the country, just above the subsistence level. Even when food was available, for the ordinary English it was just bread and cheese, with some fish if the village lived near a river. "We seldome eat to please the palate, or satisfie appetite," a countryman wrote, "onely eate to live, give nature her due."

The lack of trees due to centuries of over-cutting forests even made it difficult for people to heat their homes, which meant they were often cold. Kelley explains:

Only during the summer did the English keep consistently warm. They usually went about their homes and work with blue fingers and chapped lips....Even New England looked warm. "Here," wrote a New Englander, "we have plentie of Fire to warme us ... nay all Europe is not able to afford to make so great Fires as New-England."

John Lawson, the colony's surveyor, was sympathetic to Native Americans. "They are really better to us than we have been to them," Lawson wrote of Indians, but he also stated that "they are very vengeful, and never forget an injury done, 'till they have received Satisfaction."[27] True to Lawson's assessment, in 1711 the Tuscarora and several other tribes attacked settlers because of the continued injustices against them. Lawson and von Graffenried were captured in an isolated incident that preceded all-out war. The Swiss leader was spared, but Lawson was killed September 10, while arguing with his captors.

At dawn on September 22, the Tuscarora and their allies attacked settlements from the Neuse River to the Pamlico River, and in just a few hours killed some 130 colonists, captured about thirty prisoners, and destroyed homes and crops. Christopher Gale described the carnage in a letter seeking help from other colonies:

> On Saturday the 22d of September last, was perpetrated the grossest piece of villainy that was ever heard of in English America . . . what spectacle can strike a man with more horror and stir up more to revenge, than to see so much barbarity practiced in so little a time and so unexpectedly.[28]

The massive attack by five hundred Indians resulted in death and destruction on a scale never before experienced in North Carolina. Although the Tuscarora were joined by the Coree, Pamlico,

In 1711, several tribes of Native Americans captured John Lawson (left) and Christoph von Graffenried. Von Graffenried was released but Lawson was killed while arguing with his captors.

The pirate crew of Blackbeard's ship drinks and dances on the Carolina coast. Blackbeard's piracy caused economic hardship for the Carolina colonists.

Machapunga, and Bear River tribes, they were eventually defeated by a force of whites and nearly five hundred Indians friendly to colonists, mostly members of the Yamassee tribe. The fighting continued periodically through 1715 as several tribes desperately tried to push back the invading colonists.

In 1715 the warring tribes signed peace treaties that ended the fighting and confined them to reservations, thus eliminating one of the major obstacles to the colony's growth. But another danger soon arose, this time from the sea.

Pirates

North Carolina's development was threatened again in 1717 by pirates such as Edward Teach, who is better known as Blackbeard. After English authorities drove the pirates out of the Caribbean, where they had been looting for many years, the buccaneers moved north to the American colonies. North Carolina became a favored raiding spot because its Outer Banks, with their hidden inlets and twisting passages, made it easy for them to prey on unsuspecting ships and to elude officials trying to arrest them.

The predatory tactics of Teach, "Gentleman" Stede Bonnet, and other pirates disrupted shipping, causing economic hardship for

Carolina residents. In May 1718 Teach blockaded Charleston Harbor, cutting off shipping until officials accepted his demand for medical treatment for his crew. In his 1724 pirate history, Captain Charles Johnson claimed Blackbeard received his infamous nickname "from that large quantity of hair which, like a frightful meteor, covered his whole face and frightened America more than any comet that has appeared there [in] a long time."[29]

Despite his crimes, Teach in 1716 was allowed to build a home in Bath, and in June 1718 Governor Charles Eden pardoned him

Lieutenant Robert M. Maynard killed Blackbeard in a sword duel in November 1718, eliminating a major threat to the growth of the Carolina colony.

for his offenses. When Teach returned to piracy, the British decided to capture him, and on November 22, 1718, Lieutenant Robert M. Maynard killed him in a sword duel while their ships battled near Ocracoke Island. The British navy drove other pirates away to make the sea lanes safe again for shipping.

But geography, Native Americans, and even pirates were not the fledgling colony's worst problem. The greatest hindrance to North Carolina's continued growth came from the members of royalty who ruled it.

Lords Proprietors

The lords proprietors owned Carolina from 1663 until 1729, when the Crown reclaimed the colony because they had governed it so poorly. In 1729 North Carolina was America's most sparsely settled colony, with about thirty-five thousand people living mostly along the coast. Historian Blackwell P. Robinson explains how the proprietors mismanaged North Carolina:

> The failure of the Proprietors to establish a strong, stable, and efficient government was a great handicap to [its] growth and progress. Some of its governors were weak and ineffective, some were unscrupulous, most were unsatisfactory; hence the governors failed to preserve order, promote the welfare of the people, or defend the colony against Indians and pirates.[30]

Colonists believed the proprietors and the officials they appointed were more interested in profiting from the colony through excessive taxes and fees than governing it wisely, and they freely protested unjust laws and crooked or inept administrators. North Carolinians succeeded in forcing the removal of six governors because of their poor, sometimes corrupt leadership. In *The Atlantic Frontier: Colonial American Civilization [1607–1763]*, historian Louis B. Wright explains this attitude: "North Carolina was especially turbulent and restive under proprietary rule. To a frontier population without much respect for law at best [any act that] looked like tyranny . . . was liable to evoke a storm of disapproval and complaint."[31]

The Lords Proprietors

The original eight lords proprietors received the grant to Carolina because King Charles II owed them for helping him reclaim the English throne. The Stuarts succeeded Queen Elizabeth as monarchs of Britain, but Charles I was beheaded in 1649 and Oliver Cromwell ruled for several years. When Charles II returned the Stuarts to the throne in 1660 to end a bitter civil war, he rewarded his loyal supporters by granting them a large chunk of the New World.

Seal of the lords proprietors of Carolina. The proprietors ruled Carolina for sixty-six years.

The eight lords proprietors were Edward Hyde, earl of Clarendon; George Monck, duke of Albemarle; William Craven, earl of Craven; John Lord Berkeley; Anthony Ashley Cooper, earl of Shaftesbury; Sir George Carteret; Sir William Berkeley, governor of Virginia; and Sir John Colleton. But in The Proprietors of Carolina, *William S. Powell explains that they were only the first to hold the title:*

During the sixty-six years of proprietary control nearly fifty different persons served as Proprietors or were entitled to do so. For long periods several of the shares were in dispute resulting in great confusion as to which individuals were entitled to seats at the proprietary table. There were even several women who owned or claimed to own shares.

Powell notes that few proprietors were qualified to fulfill their duties as absentee landlords of a fledgling New World colony:

The Proprietors surely had slight understanding of the colonial territory over which they held such power. It may be that by sheer numbers—*eight* Proprietors—the problems were magnified. At any rate, confusion reigned in Carolina more or less continually for as long as the Lords Proprietors remained in charge.

One of the governors forced out of office was Seth Sothel, who became a proprietor in 1667 when he bought the share in the colony originally owned by Henry Hyde. One of the most corrupt and arbitrary officials to ever rule a British colony, Sothel was governor from 1683 to 1689. He was removed from office after the colony's legislature found him guilty of thirteen charges, including illegally seizing property, accepting bribes, and imprisoning his opponents without trial.

One of the few smart moves the proprietors made was to divide Carolina in half. The northern part of Carolina was called Albemarle until 1691, when proprietors appointed a deputy governor for the area that they named North Carolina. People living there became angry, however, because proprietors were spending more money to develop what was now called South Carolina. The proprietors did this because the southern half included Charleston, which had a good harbor and was profiting from sea trade. In *A History of the American People*, Paul Johnson explains that this dissension forced proprietors to divide the colony:

> In the Carolinas there was constant bickering between north and south. In 1691 the Carolina proprietors recognized the *fait accompli* of a northern region by dividing the colony into two provinces, with a deputy governor living in the town of Albemarle, capital of what was already being called North Carolina. On May 12, 1712, the separation was completed and North Carolina had became a colony on its own. It had already run its own legislature, be it noted, for forty-seven years—five years longer than South Carolina's in Charleston.[32]

A Royal Colony

The lords proprietors were such inept leaders that on July 25, 1729, King George II bought back the colony, paying seventy-five thousand pounds apiece for each of their shares. Sir George Carteret, later to become the earl of Granville, refused to relinquish his share but gave up the right to govern land he would own until the Revolutionary

Two lords proprietors disagree over how to manage North Carolina's religious laws. The lords proprietors were criticized often for their poor management, and the English government reclaimed the colony in 1729.

War. Historians Hugh T. Lefler and William S. Powell explain that becoming a royal colony stabilized North Carolina:

The Crown [the king] merely replaced the lords proprietors as the immediate source of power. There was, however, a definite change in the spirit and efficiency of the government. A strong executive capable of sustained policy succeeded a weak and constantly changing leadership, and this made possible a stability of purpose, promptness of action, and a strength of administration that had been [previously] impossible.[33]

For example, Governor George Burrington, who took office in 1731, extended a road across the colony from Virginia to Cape Fear, which improved communication and transportation and made it easier to settle the Cape Fear Valley. His successor, Gabriel Johnston, took the even bolder step of exempting newcomers from public taxes for ten years as a way to lure new citizens.

The Colony Grows

North Carolina experienced explosive growth as a royal colony, and by 1775 its population had swollen to nearly 350,000, making it the fourth largest colony. North Carolina governor Arthur Dobbs in 1766 wrote, "This province is settling faster than any on the continent. Last autumn and winter, upwards of one thousand wagons passed thro' Salisbury with families from the northward to settle in this province chiefly." Just two years later a South Carolina newspaper noted, "There is scarce any history either ancient or modern, which affords an account of such a rapid and sudden increase of inhabitants in a back frontier country, as that of North Carolina."[34]

During the royal era, people from other colonies who migrated to North Carolina were joined by a tidal wave of emigrants from Scotland, Germany, Wales, England, Ireland, and other countries. Historian Curtis Nettels explains that most were trying to escape economic hardship or various forms of persecution:

To the poor peasants and workers of Europe, immersed in poverty, war, and religious persecution, the English colonies beckoned with an irresistible appeal. There at least one might enjoy peace and security, freedom of Protestant worship, and the economic opportunity of cheap land and high wages: there perhaps one might pass beyond the grasp of the tax-collector and the sound of marching armies.[35]

So many people arrived that within a few years North Carolina's population surpassed that of South Carolina, which had always been bigger and more successful. The newcomers filled up coastal areas and the Cape Fear Valley and then moved ever westward, reaching the mountains by the 1760s and then pushing up and over them in search of new land and new opportunities. New Bern was rebuilt and many new communities were started including Halifax, Hillsborough, Salisbury, Salem, Charlotte, and Wilmington, the colony's main port, which was founded in 1730.

As North Carolina grew, however, the Crown had to create more counties, the basic unit of government, and name new judges, sheriffs, and tax collectors. Although the colony's royal governors after 1729 were generally fair and honest, many of the local officials they appointed were inefficient and corrupt, levying excessive and unfair taxes, accepting bribes, and violating the rights of citizens. North Carolinians had never been shy about fighting injustices done by the lords proprietors, and they now began banding together to stand up for their rights against crown officials.

The Regulators

In 1768 people living in the colony's western counties formed the Regulators, a vigilante group that sought to reform government. One of their demands in a written message on May 21, 1768, was to end "the corrupt and arbitrary practices of nefarious and designing men who . . . use every artifice, every fraud, and where these fail, threats and menaces to squeeze and extort [money] from the wretched poor."[36] They also complained that the colony spent too much money from 1767 to 1770 to build a governor's residence in New Bern, which they dubbed "Tryon's Palace" after Governor William Tryon.

When their efforts to achieve reforms peacefully through petitions and negotiations failed, Regulators in Orange, Edgecome, Anson, and Johnston Counties withheld taxes and staged protests, some of which evolved into riots. On October 5, 1770, Regulators stormed the courthouse in Hillsborough, dragged a local judge from his bench, and destroyed his court. The worst violence came on May 16, 1771, at Great Alamance Creek when about two thousand Regulators fought a force of fourteen hundred militia soldiers led by Tryon, who was on his way to Hillsborough for a special court session; he brought the soldiers along to protect the court and suppress Regulators.

The Battle of Alamance was one-sided, and the poorly equipped, ill-trained Regulators were easily defeated. Tryon's victory ended the movement as a dozen Regulators were convicted of treason (six were hanged), more than sixty-four hundred applied for pardons, and others fled west beyond North Carolina's borders. The show of force, for a time, had quelled the colony's rebellious tendencies.

A Fighting Spirit

When historians more than a century later began to consider the significance of the Battle of Alamance, they romantically

The Regulators, a vigilante group seeking government reform, objected to the leadership of Governor William Tryon (left center).

Governor William Tryon directs his English soldiers to suppress the rebellious Regulators at the Battle of Alamance.

proclaimed it the opening salvo of the American Revolution: Historian John H. Wheeler wrote that it accounted for "the first blood spilled in these United States in resistance to oppression by the English government."[37] Later assessments rejected that idea, claiming it was a revolt against unfair colonial rule and not Great Britain. Either interpretation was proof that North Carolinians were not afraid to stand up for their rights.

Chapter Three

Life in Colonial North Carolina

John Lawson was one of the colony's most influential settlers, a surveyor who explored the entire area, mapped out new towns, and knew as much about life in North Carolina's early years as anyone. In his 1709 *History of Carolina*, Lawson wrote that it was a good place to make a home: "The Inhabitants of Carolina, through the richness of the soil, live an easy and pleasant life."[38]

In fact, it appeared to be so easy to live well in North Carolina that residents of neighboring Virginia began to be envious, and a rivalry developed between the two colonies. William Byrd II of Virginia traveled throughout North Carolina in 1728 while helping survey their border to resolve long-standing boundary disputes; King George II had demanded this be done because he was preparing to buy back North Carolina from the lords proprietors. Byrd came to believe that even lazy people could live well in North Carolina:

Tis a thorough Aversion to Labor that makes People file off to North Carolina, where Plenty and a Warm sun confirm them in their Disposition ... here People may live plentifully at a Triffleing expense. ... Surely there is no place in the World where the Inhabitants live with less Labour than in North Carolina.[39]

Byrd's comments were undoubtedly tinged with resentment that the final boundary line surrendered all of the disputed territory to

While preparing to buy North Carolina from the lords proprietors, King George II (pictured) sent William Byrd to survey the colony's borders. Byrd inaccurately claimed that the colonists lived well with little effort.

North Carolina's Colonial System of Government

Although the colony of North Carolina was owned at first by the lords proprietors and later by the king of England, its residents were granted a strong role in governing their home in the New World. Its system of government was basically the same under both the lords proprietors and the Crown. The following explanation of this system of government is from the North Carolina Encyclopedia, *a publication of the State Library of North Carolina available on the Internet (www.statelibrary.dcr.state. nc.us/nc/history/history.html).*

Colonial government in North Carolina was essentially the same during both the proprietary and royal periods. The only major difference was who appointed colonial officials. There were two primary units of government: one consisted of the governor and his council and the other consisted of a colonial assembly of persons elected by the qualified voters of the county. There were also colonial courts; however, unlike today's courts, they were rarely involved in formulating policy. All colonial officials were

North Carolina, but the reality of life in colonial North Carolina was much different. People who moved there could live well, but only if they worked very hard.

Early Life

People began moving into Carolina from Virginia in the 1650s. Farmers searching for fertile land, hunters and trappers seeking game, and traders who wanted to buy animal skins all followed navigable streams from southeastern Virginia into the area that would one day become North Carolina. It was the farmers who brought their families and built homes through backbreaking labor who would really tame this wonderful new land. Historian H. G. Jones explains how these rugged settlers lived while carving a home out of the wilderness:

appointed by either the Lords Proprietors prior to 1729 or the Crown afterwards. Members of the colonial assembly were elected from the various precincts (counties) and from certain towns which had been granted representation. The term "precinct" as a geographical unit ceased to exist after 1735. These areas became known as "counties."

The governor was an appointed official, as were the colonial secretary, attorney general, surveyor general, and the receiver general. All officials served at the pleasure of the Lords Proprietors or the Crown [the king]. During the proprietary period, the council was comprised of appointed persons who were to look after the proprietors' interests in the New World. The council served as an advisory group to the governor during the proprietary and royal periods, as well as serving as the upper house of the legislature when the assembly was in session. When vacancies occurred in colonial offices or on the council, the governor was authorized to carry out all mandates of the proprietors, and could make a temporary appointment until the vacancy was filled by proprietary or royal commission. One member of the council was chosen as president of the group, and many council members were also colonial officials.

With hand implements [they] felled trees, built cabins, cleared lands and cultivated crops. Guns provided them meat and protection. Horses were few, and while oxen were trained for simple chores, human labor performed most of the tasks. Clothing, household furniture, farm implements, and canoes were made by hand. Basic foods—corn, wheat, and pork—were grown on each farm. A variety of wildlife yielded furs and skins, and trees provided logs for cabins and wood for fires.[40]

Life was hard and they faced many problems and many dangers, from bad weather and illness to attacks by Native Americans angry that their ancestral homeland was being invaded. One thing they did not have to fear, however, was going hungry. The New World had a

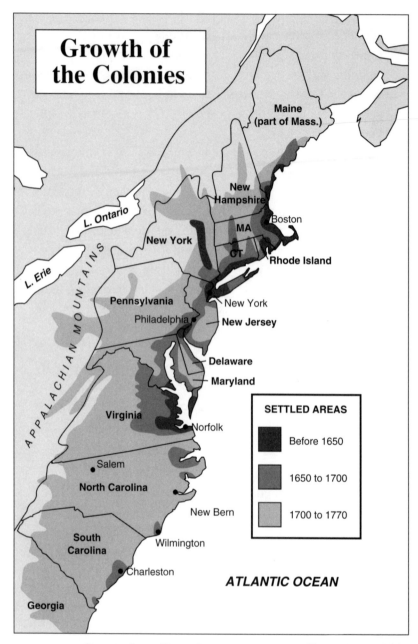

Growth of the Colonies

Maine
(part of Mass.)

New
Hampshire

L. Ontario

New York

Boston

MA

CT

Rhode Island

L. Erie

APPALACHIAN MOUNTAINS

Pennsylvania

New York

Philadelphia

New Jersey

Delaware

Maryland

Virginia

Norfolk

Salem

North Carolina

New Bern

South
Carolina

Wilmington

Charleston

Georgia

SETTLED AREAS

Before 1650

1650 to 1700

1700 to 1770

ATLANTIC OCEAN

temperate climate that allowed two crops annually, an incredible bounty for farmers accustomed to cold weather that limited them to one harvest. The wilderness also teemed with wildlife, including buffalo that roamed forest areas in the colony's early years. Historian R. D. W. Connor believes, "It was the presence of an unlimited food supply in the forests that enabled the pioneers to push out into the wilderness and prepare the way for civilization."[41]

As more and more settlers moved to North Carolina, towns began to grow up. The first towns were built along rivers and became commercial centers. As more and more communities began to emerge, the fledgling colony was gradually transformed from a wilderness to a settled area.

Colonial Society

One of the reasons people immigrated to America was the opportunity it offered them for equality. In Great Britain and other countries, members of royalty who had inherited wealth and power from their families controlled their nations politically and economically, and average people had little hope of becoming richer, rising socially, or creating a better life for themselves. But in North Carolina, everyone who worked hard could become prosperous and improve the way they and their families lived.

Despite the New World's lure of equality, however, class distinctions existed in North Carolina and other colonies that were similar to those that people had endured in their homelands, which were still ruled by people with wealth and royal titles. In *Colonial North Carolina*, Hugh T. Lefler and William S. Powell explain this social structure:

> Colonial North Carolinians lived in a class-conscious society. The idea that some men were socially superior while others were socially inferior was recognized in the colony just as it was in [Europe]. The pattern of class structure was not, however, absolutely rigid [as in Europe]; sometimes a sturdy middle-class family would ascend the scale, and it is certainly true that members of the upper class not infrequently fell from their lofty positions in the social order.[42]

The upper class that developed in North Carolina included royalty, the clergy, doctors and other professional workers, large landowners, and government officials. This elite group accounted

The majority of North Carolina's settlers made their living from agriculture. The colony's major cash crop was tobacco.

for only 5 percent of the colony's citizens and was sometimes called the "planter class" even though people with large estates were not its only members. Although most plantations were smaller than 500 acres, some people had thousands, like "King" Roger Moore, who owned 10,000 acres in the Cape Fear Valley, and Governor Johnston, who laid claim to 24,000 acres.

One step below this elite level was the small farm class, people who owned their own land and thus had the right to vote; this group encompassed by far the largest number of North Carolinians. Another step lower were subsistence farmers, roaming hunters and trappers, unskilled laborers, and "Christian servants," men and women who were indentured servants.

At the bottom of the social scale came African Americans, whether free or slave, and Native Americans. Because North Carolina did not have many large plantations, it had fewer slaves than other southern colonies, and its slaves never made up more than 25 percent of its total population compared to South Carolina's 60 percent.

North Carolina's Economy

Regardless of social class, nearly everyone in North Carolina made a living through agriculture. At least 95 percent of the colony's early settlers were engaged in farming or related industries, a natural development because of its abundant, fertile, and cheap land and the necessity for people to grow their own food. The major crops were corn, tobacco, peas, beans, wheat, and rice, and for much of the eighteenth century North Carolina produced so much food that it was known as the "breadbasket" of the colonies. The colony's major cash crop was tobacco, the use of which Sir Walter Raleigh helped popularize in England, and by 1772 planters were shipping more than 1.5 million pounds of it annually to Europe.

Colonial farming was primitive and environmentally unsound. When farmers exhausted the soil by continually growing crops in the same fields, they simply cleared more land to replace the depleted acreage. In 1775 the anonymous author of *American Husbandry* described this wasteful technique:

The mode of common husbandry [farming] is to break up a piece of land, a work very easily done. . . . [T]his they sow with Indian corn for several years successively, till it will yield crops no longer. . . . [W]hen the land is pretty well exhausted they sow it with peas and beans once a year and afterwards sow it with wheat for two or three years. In this system of crops they change the land as fast as it wears out, clearing fresh pieces of wood land [and] exhausting them in succession.[43]

Although North Carolina did not have much livestock in its early years, over time the number of cattle, hogs, chickens, and other domestic animals in the colony increased. Eventually, bigger landowners had herds of a thousand or more cows, giving North

Carolina adequate supplies of meat, leather, and other animal products.

North Carolina was not a major shipping colony because of its lack of good ports, but it developed a thriving secondary business related to the sea. The colony's leading commercial industry was manufacturing tar, pitch, rosin, and turpentine, which were collectively termed "naval stores" because they were used on ships. England had previously relied on Scandinavian countries for naval stores, but from 1720 to 1870 North Carolina led the world in their production. Naval stores were processed from trees in the colony's extensive forests, which also helped North Carolina become a leading source of lumber products such as barrel staves, shingles, and boards.

The Colony's Culture

During the era of crown rule, the riches North Carolina's economy produced helped raise the standard of living for almost everyone. Homes became larger and more comfortable, with finer furniture and other amenities, and life improved in many ways: more churches were started; James Davis brought the first printing press to the colony and in 1751 began publishing the *North Carolina Gazette,* its first newspaper; and schools and libraries were opened.

North Carolina, however, was never considered as refined or cultured as many other colonies. For example, it did not have a widespread public school system until the middle of the eighteenth century, which meant that many of its residents were illiterate. In *A History of the South,* William B. Hesseltine writes:

> While North Carolina developed politically until it was the most democratic of the Southern colonies of the colonial period, its cultural and social development lagged behind that of the other colonies. The colony had few libraries and no colleges, though Edenton and a few other places had schools.[44]

The colony's slow cultural progress was partly due to the fact that it had fewer big plantations and large cities than neighboring

In comparison to those in other colonies, the homes of North Carolinians were humble. The homes of people living in the mountains were simple and made of timber.

colonies like Virginia or South Carolina. It was the plantation owners and businessmen in large cities who became rich enough to be able to send their children to colleges and universities, to engage in cultural pursuits such as learning to play musical instruments, and to subsidize development of schools and libraries. And while rich Virginia planters built costly mansions such as Thomas Jefferson's famed Monticello, in North Carolina, plantation homes were much more humble. John Bricknell, an Edenton physician, describes plantation houses during the 1730s:

The most substantial Planters generally use Brick, and Lime, which is made of Oyster-shells, for there are no Stones to be found proper for that purposes, but near the Mountains; the meaner [poorer] sort erect [homes] with Timber, the outside with Clap-Boards, the Roofs of both sorts of Houses are made with Shingles, and they generally have Sash Windows, and affect large and decent Rooms with good Closets.[45]

Virginians especially tended to view their southern neighbors as unrefined, often ridiculing North Carolinians as "idle debtors," "theeves," "pyrates," and "runaway servants."[46] In 1775 when Janet Schaw came from Scotland to Wilmington to visit her brother, she agreed with that assessment. She claimed men she met lacked education and social graces, a lack of refinement she attributed to the way the earliest North Carolinians had raised their children:

> As the father found the labours of his boys necessary to him, he led them to the woods, and taught the sturdy lad to glory in the stroke he could give with his Ax, in the trees he felled, and the deer he shot; to [hunt] the wolf, the bear and the Alligator; and to guard his habitation from Indian inroads was most justly his pride. But a few generations this way lost every art or science, which their fathers might have brought out, and tho' necessity no longer prescribed these severe occupations, custom has established it as still necessary for the men to spend their time aboard in the fields; and to be a good marksman is the highest ambition of the youth.[47]

However, it was North Carolina's great middle class, composed mostly of the small farmers Schaw thought were uncouth, which gave the colony its distinctive character. Historian R. D. W. Connor provides a portrait of the farmer class, whose members generally owned between fifty and two hundred acres and led simple lives:

> A strong, fearless, independent race, simple in taste, crude in manners, provincial in outlook, democratic in social relations, tenacious of their rights, sensitive to encroachments on their personal liberties, and, when interested in religion at all, earnest, narrow, and dogmatic.[48]

Religion was a contentious issue in North Carolina, whose citizens rejected an attempt by the lords proprietors to establish the

Anglican Church, England's state church, as the colony's official religion. Many people had moved to America to escape religious persecution, so Quakers, Baptists, Presbyterians, Lutherans, and members of other Protestant sects refused to acknowledge the Anglican Church as superior to their own.

It was only natural, however, that many North Carolinians would reject England's official church, because tens of thousands of its residents were from other countries, notably Scotland and Germany. These newcomers brought with them new attitudes and new traditions that slowly began to exert a great influence on North Carolina's development.

The Scotch

In 1732 shiploads of Scottish Highlanders began arriving by the hundreds at the port of Wilmington; more Scots immigrated directly to North Carolina than any other nationality. The Scots traveled ninety miles up the Cape Fear River to Cross Creek to make their homes, and by 1762 so many had congregated in the area that they founded a second community, Campbelltown, whose name reflected their Scottish roots. (In 1783 the two towns were combined and renamed Fayetteville after the Marquis de Lafayette, the French hero of the American Revolution.)

In their new home, Highlanders honored old traditions by wearing kilts, typical Scottish dress the English had banned, and speaking Gaelic. The Cape Fear Valley became known as "Little Scotland," and as late as 1828 a tourist in Fayetteville commented that for miles around, everybody spoke Gaelic. Besides introducing Gaelic to the colony, the Scots brought their own unique form of music. Writing in the 1730s, Edenton physician John Bricknell said of the Scots: "Dancing they are all fond of, especially when they can get a Fiddle, or Bag-pipe; at this they will continue Hours together, nay, so attach'd are they to this darling Amusmennt, that if they can't procure Musick, they will sing for themselves."[49]

Another large group of newcomers was the Scotch Irish, who were racially Scotch but geographically Irish. They were descendants of Scots sent to Northern Ireland in the early seventeenth century by English monarchs to supplant the Irish, who opposed English rule. The Scotch Irish had been successful in Ireland, but many moved to America so they could live more freely. Famed frontiersman Daniel Boone was among the most famous of North Carolina's Scotch Irish, an ethnic group that would produce two

Religious Freedom and the Moravians

Many people came to North Carolina and other colonies seeking religious freedom. These groups included the Scottish Highlanders, who were Presbyterian, as well as Baptists, Quakers, Lutherans, German Reformed, Methodists, and the Moravians. In North Carolina: The History of a Southern State, *Hugh Talmadge Lefler and Albert Ray Newsome explain how the Moravians established their church-based community:*

In the fall of [1752] Moravian Bishop August Gottlieb Spangenberg, with a party of Brethren from Pennsylvania, visited the colony to select a place for settlement. They traversed North Carolina from Edenton to the Blue Ridge and finally chose a site in what is now Forsyth County. Spangenberg, well pleased with the land, climate, abundant game, and other resources, regarded it "as a corner which the land had reserved for the Brethren." ... The first group of settlers arrived at a spot where now stands the community of Bethabara. This party consisted of fifteen unmarried men [including a] minister, physician, baker, tailor, shoemaker, tanner, gardener, three farmers, and two carpenters. Their first shelter was the deserted cabin of a German trapper, Hans Wagoner. Within a short time they had begun a town and before the end of the following year they had in operation a carpenter shop, a flour mill, a pottery, a cooperage works, a tanner, a blacksmith shop, and a shoe shop. The Moravians tended to segregate themselves from other settlements. They were determined to preserve their religious, social, and economic customs. They emphasized community cooperation and common ownership of property. It was not until 1849 that the congregation abandoned its supervision of business, and not until 1856 that the lease system [to own property] was dropped.

presidents born in North Carolina: James Polk and Andrew Johnson. Historian Blackwell P. Robinson claims the Scotch Irish played an important role in settling North Carolina:

They established Presbyterian churches throughout a wide area. Within a short time they established schools. They developed agriculture and a variety of industries. They had a flair for politics, and they had fighting qualities acquired in their rough, hardy, outdoor life, which [helped] them on the frontier.[50]

Germans

Often, Scots who moved to North Carolina were descendants of people who originally settled other colonies. Many transplanted Scots came from Pennsylvania, which also contributed thousands of new residents with a quite different heritage. Pennsylvania was home to many German immigrants, and in the mid-1700s hundreds began moving to North Carolina. The Germans belonged to three main Protestant sects—Lutheran, Reformed, and the Moravians, who were also known as the United Brethren and were one of the most influential German groups to come to North Carolina.

In 1752 the leader of the Moravians in Bethlehem, Pennsylvania, Bishop August Gottlieb Spangenberg, began searching for a site to expand his church community. He chose the Piedmont, where he bought 98,985 acres from the earl of Granville, and named the land Wachovia after an area in Germany. On November 17, 1753, the first fifteen Moravians arrived at the site chosen for a new town, which they named Bethabara, meaning "House of Passage." As more Moravians arrived, Bethabara grew and church members in 1759 founded Bethania and in 1766 Salem, which was located in the center of Wachovia and would eventually develop into the city known today as Winston-Salem.

The Moravians were unlike any other North Carolinians. But although they spoke a different language (German) and had many customs that seemed strange to their new neighbors, they were accepted because they were industrious, honest, and had many fine craftsmen. The biggest difference between the Moravians and other North Carolinians was how they lived. In organizing the new town, Spangenberg decided people should live communally because he feared so many would be unequipped to live alone in the wilderness:

> What will happen to those who do not have the necessary talents [for the frontier]? To speak plainly, among fifty members brought up in our congregation or who have lived with us some years, there is probably not one who could maintain himself alone in the forest. Perhaps it would be wise to settle six or ten families together, each in its own house, all working together under a capable overseer.[51]

Settlers living in the mountains of North Carolina. The independent spirit of the colonists led them to participate in the battle for freedom from English rule.

Independent Spirit

But whether North Carolinians traced their roots back to England, Scotland, Germany, or some other far-off land, historian Joanne Young maintains that they almost uniformly shared one key belief: "The people of North Carolina were from the beginning [of the colony] inclined toward individualism and democracy; they seemed always to feel that 'the government is best which governs least.'"[52] North Carolinians simply wanted to live in freedom and have the right to govern themselves. It was a belief that would lead North Carolina to participate in the American Revolution.

Chapter Four

North Carolina in the Revolutionary War

The original relationship between Great Britain and the men and women who began populating America was similar to the bond that exists between parents and small children; the mother country supplied them with necessities such as food and, like a stern parent, taught them how to behave by establishing and controlling local government. Paul Johnson claims in *A History of the American People* that even in the early 1700s, a time when the colonies had already matured and begun to develop their own leaders, "colonists still had the look homeward reflex and saw the crown as their father and savior."[53]

But gradually, people in North Carolina and other colonies realized they were becoming self-sufficient from Great Britain. Americans, as these British subjects were beginning to call themselves, began to resent being governed by a king who was far away and who, they firmly believed, cared more about taxing them to fill his treasury than helping them settle a new land. Many colonists, however, found it difficult to surrender their loyalty to Great Britain, and when the Revolution began, not all Americans wanted their freedom. Historians generally believe that a third of colonists, called Patriots or Whigs, backed the battle for independence, another third, termed Loyalists or Tories, wanted to remain under British control, and the remainder were undecided.

This division was especially dramatic in North Carolina, where, historians Hugh Talmadge Lefler and Albert Ray Newsome explain, "The Revolution became a civil war—Whigs against Tories, neighbor against neighbor, and sometimes brother against brother."[54] But even though some North Carolinians opposed revolution, the colony that was the site of the first English attempt to establish a presence in the New World was also one of the first to take up the fight for freedom.

Unfair Taxation

Relations between Great Britain and its colonies began to deteriorate in 1763 after the English won the French and Indian War. The victory more than doubled England's New World holdings—it gained Canada and the eastern half of the Mississippi Valley from France and Florida from Spain, France's ally. But because the war had emptied the royal treasury, the British passed a series of new taxes to increase revenue. Instead, the measures set Americans on the path to revolution.

The new taxes levied on sugar and currency in 1764 did not create much opposition in North Carolina, but passage of the Stamp Act in March 1765 ignited violent protests. The stamps, which created a tax on paper items, were supposed to be affixed to legal documents, newspapers, and even playing cards. But because their elected officials had not approved the tax, Americans believed it violated the principle of English liberty that guaranteed no taxation without representation.

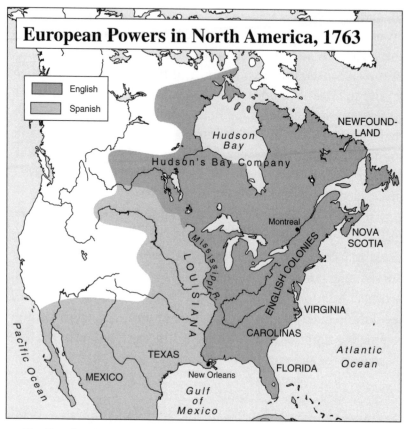

European Powers in North America, 1763

By October 1765 angry North Carolinians were protesting the tax in Wilmington, New Bern, and Cross Creek, and the Sons of Liberty, colonists who wanted their independence from Great Britain, were forming local chapters. On November 29, armed protesters refused to allow a ship carrying the stamps to land at Brunswick, which meant officials had none to place on paper items. The protests ended in February 1766 when an armed group confronted Governor William Tryon and demanded that he not use the stamps. He relented, in what historian Jeffrey J. Crow claims was a huge victory for North Carolinians:

> Thus, the Sons of Liberty successfully resisted the Stamp Act. The protesters had been led by gentlemen, planters, and merchants. The threat of mob violence and even rebellion throughout the colonies [similar protests were

held in other areas] had compelled the British to back down, for Parliament soon repealed the Stamp Act.[55]

The failure of the Stamp Act was the beginning of the end of British rule in America, and in no other colony had resistance to it been as forceful or well executed as in North Carolina. Parliament, however, soon approved more taxes and laws that infuriated colonists. The final indignity was the Tea Act of 1773.

Independence Now!

Angry colonists in Boston and other cities destroyed tea shipments so they would not have to pay the hated new tax, but in North Carolina there was a different type of protest. On October 25, 1774, fifty-one women from five counties met in Edenton at the home of Elizabeth King and agreed to honor a plea by the colony's First Provincial Congress to stop buying tea and other British goods. The "Edenton Tea Party" is considered the earliest known political action ever taken by American women.

Reproductions of revenue stamps the English government required on paper products. Protest of the Stamp Act was the colonies' first act of revolution.

Members of the North Carolina Assembly had wanted to elect delegates to the Continental Congress in Philadelphia, where the colonies intended to discuss their growing concerns over British rule, but Governor Josiah Martin refused to allow the Assembly to meet. Assembly leader John Harvey's response was, "In that case, the people will hold a convention independent of the governor."[56] Harvey and other colonial leaders decided to hold the First Provincial Congress, a meeting attended by representatives from thirty

The Edenton Tea Party

In 1774 after North Carolina's First Provincial Congress decided to protest the Tea Act by refusing to buy any more English tea, a group of women pledged their support for the rebellious action. In North Carolina: The First Two Hundred Years, *Joanne Young describes what is believed to be the first recorded political act by colonial women:*

All of this had been men's work, but women in the colony were also involved. It was they who had to find a substitute for British tea. Well, there was sassafras in abundance, which made a lovely spicy red brew, and yaupon, a variety of holly, the Indians of the Outer Banks had used to make a golden tea. In Edenton, a group of women were determined to state their support [of the ban on buying tea]. Tradition says they were headed by Penelope Barker, wife of colonial agent Thomas, and that the "Edenton Tea Party" was held at the home of Mrs. Elizabeth King, whose home [stood near] the handsome red brick Chowan County Courthouse. The day was October 25, 1774, and likely a balmy Indian summer afternoon which allowed them to gather in the Kings' garden, for few houses in Edenton could have entertained fifty-one ladies in their parlors! One by one they signed their names to the agreement "to do everything as far as lies in our power to testify to our sincere adherence" to those resolves.

When the news was reported in London's Morning Chronicle, *however, Young admits the reaction to the stand the women took was typical of the era's male chauvinism:*

Arthur Iredell, who read it there, wrote at once to his brother James, a young Edenton lawyer: "Is there a female Congress in Edenton, too? I hope not, for we Englishmen are afraid of the male Congress, but if the ladies, who have ever been esteemed the most formidable enemies, should attack us, the most fatal consequence is to be dreaded." The only hope he could see was that probably few places in America "possess so much female artillery as Edenton."

counties and four towns, many of whom were also members of the Assembly.

The First Provincial Congress in New Bern on August 25, 1774, is considered historic as the first elected assembly held in America in defiance of the Crown. The First Provincial Congress protested unfair taxation, proposed ways to fight it, and elected William Hooper, Richard Caswell, and Joseph Hewes as delegates to the Continental Congress, which unified the colonies in their fight for independence.

Events then moved quickly toward war with Great Britain, and North Carolinians helped lead the way. As far back as 1760, Governor Arthur Dobbs had complained that "a rising spirit of independency"[57] was spreading through the colony, and after the Revolution began on April 19, 1775, in Massachusetts with the Battles of Lexington and Concord, North Carolina was quick to join the fray.

On May 20 (a date emblazoned today on the state flag), members of the Mecklenburg County Committee of Safety signed the "Mecklenburg Declaration of Independence." (Committees of Safety had sprung up throughout North Carolina and other colonies to work for independence.) It is not known exactly what the document said because it has not survived, but various historical accounts claim it protested unfair taxation, condemned Martin, and called North Carolinians "a free and independent people."[58]

Although historians still debate whether it was the first formal "Declaration of Independence" from Great Britain, Mecklenburgers soon proved again they wanted to be free. On May 31, the Committee of Safety met in Charlotte and approved a series of resolutions, which have survived, that recommended electing military officers "who shall hold and exercise their several powers by virtue of this choice and independent of the Crown of Great Britain and former constitution of this Province" and declared anyone who accepts an office from the Crown "an enemy to his country."[59] North Carolinians were ready to fight for their freedom.

Divided Loyalties

Despite the many calls for independence in Mecklenburg and other North Carolina communities, the American Revolution divided the former colony. The Patriots included most of the small farmers and some plantation owners while the Tories, also called King's Men or Royalists, were mainly wealthy merchants, large landowners, government officials, and professionals such as lawyers and doctors. In North Carolina, those who remained neutral included Quakers, Moravians, and many German settlers.

The divided loyalties the Revolution created cut across social, economic, and ethnic lines, breaking up communities, friendships, and families. One irony is that two groups whose common heritage indicated they should have both hated the British—Scottish Highlanders and the Scotch Irish—fought on opposing sides. The Scotch Irish gladly warred against the British while the Highlanders decided to support the country that had taken over their homeland. Historian William S. Powell explains why the Scots backed the king:

Before leaving the Highlands, they had been required by their English masters to take an oath never again to oppose the British Crown, and an oath to them was sacred. A man's honor in the eighteenth century was precious indeed, and an oath was not to be violated under any circumstances.[60]

Patriots took control of North Carolina in the early months of the Revolution, forcing Governor Martin to flee in May from the capital in New Bern, first to Fort Johnston on Cape Fear and then in July to the protection of *Cruizer*, a British ship. From there, the man who would be North Carolina's last royal governor attempted to rally Loyalists to counterattack the Patriots. By February 1776 Martin's appeal had helped gather a force of sixteen hundred Highlanders who lived along the Cape Fear River and were led by Donald Macdonald.

Martin ordered them to go to Wilmington to join British troops and other Loyalists, including African American slaves who had been promised their freedom if they fought for England. But Patriots learned of the plan, and eleven hundred North Carolina soldiers were ordered to stop the Highlanders from crossing Moore's Creek Bridge on their way to Wilmington. The Patriots arrived at the bridge first, and on the morning of February 27 calmly awaited the first battle of the American Revolution on North Carolina soil.

To the accompaniment of shrilling bagpipes, the Scots, who had few guns but wielded traditional claymore swords, bravely charged with loud cries of "King George and Broadswords!"[61] The Patriot guns shattered the Scots, who within minutes were in full retreat. Only one Patriot was killed and one wounded while some 50 Scots were killed or wounded and 850 captured, including Macdonald and his two sons. Historian Jeffrey J. Crow writes that "the Battle of Moore's Creek Bridge accelerated the movement toward independence [in North Carolina]."[62]

North Carolinians were soon ready to take another historic step toward freedom. On April 4, 1776, eighty-three members of the Fourth Provincial Congress met at Halifax and began working on the Halifax Resolves. Approved April 12, the historic statement criticized British rule and authorized the North Carolina representative in the Continental Congress to "concur with the delegates of the other Colonies in declaring Independency."[63]

The Halifax Resolves was the first official state call for independence, having been approved a month before a similar Virginia statement. When Thomas Jefferson wrote the nation's Declaration of Independence that summer, he considered the language and sentiments of the Resolves along with similar statements by other colonies.

Establishing a State

After declaring independence, it was time for North Carolinians to begin governing themselves. The Fifth Provincial Congress convened in Halifax on November 12, 1776, and in just six weeks the 169 delegates approved North Carolina's first constitution. The short, simple document stated that citizens "ought to have the sole

The Halifax Resolves

North Carolina claims to have been the first state to call for independence from Great Britain. On April 12, 1776, the Fourth Provincial Congress meeting in Halifax unanimously approved the Halifax Resolves, which authorized its delegates to the Continental Congress to vote for independence. The following excerpts from the Halifax Resolves are from the North Carolina State Library Internet site:

The Select Committee taking into Consideration the usurpations and violences attempted and committed by the King and Parliament of Britain against America, and the further Measures to be taken for frustrating the same, and for the better defence of this province reported as follows, to wit,

It appears to your Committee that pursuant to the Plan concerted by the British Ministry for subjugating America, the King and Parliament of Great Britain have usurped a Power over the Persons and Properties of the People unlimited and uncontrolled and disregarding their humble Petitions for Peace, Liberty and Safety, have made divers Legislative Acts, denouncing War, Famine and every Species of Calamity daily employed in destroying the People and committing the most horrid devastations on the

and exclusive Right of regulating the internal Government and Police thereof," and an accompanying Declaration of Rights claimed "all political Power is vested in and derived from the People only."[64]

The constitution limited the authority of the governor—North Carolinians, after all, had fought for more than a century with the proprietary and royal governors who ruled them—and gave more strength to the General Assembly, which exercised full legislative power and chose all state executive and judicial officers. Representation in the two-house legislature was based on units of local government; voters of each county elected one representative to the senate and two members to the house of commons, while six (later seven) towns each elected one member of the house.

Country. That Governors in different Colonies have declared Protection to Slaves who should imbrue their Hands in the Blood of their Masters. That the Ships belonging to America are declared prizes of War and many of them have been violently seized and confiscated in consequence of which multitudes of the people have been destroyed or from easy Circumstances reduced to the most Lamentable distress.

And whereas the moderation hitherto manifested by the United Colonies and their sincere desire to be reconciled to the Mother Country on Constitutional Principles, have procured no mitigation of the aforesaid Wrongs and usurpations and no hopes remain of obtaining redress by those Means alone which have been hitherto tried, Your Committee are of Opinion that the house should enter into the following Resolve, to wit

Resolved that the delegates for this Colony in the Continental Congress be impowered to concur with the other delegates of the other Colonies in declaring Independency, and forming foreign Alliances, resolving to this Colony the Sole, and Exclusive right of forming a Constitution and Laws for this Colony, and of appointing delegates from time to time (under the direction of a general Representation thereof to meet the delegates of the other Colonies for such purposes as shall be hereafter pointed out.

The constitution was declared to be in force on December 18; citizens never had the opportunity to vote on it. Richard Caswell, a hero of the Battle of Moore's Creek, was chosen governor and sworn in January 16, 1777. Historian Blackwell P. Robinson explains the dire situation confronting North Carolina when the General Assembly met for the first time on April 7, in New Bern:

The new State government faced many critical problems. Troops had to be raised, organized, trained, and equipped. Additional revenues had to be raised to prosecute the war and to operate the new government. Tories had to be watched, though their ardor had been cooled by the defeat at Moore's Creek. The Cherokee Indians, who were keeping the frontier settlements in a state of constant alarm, had to be subdued. There were also the acute problems of taxes, paper currency, and inflation. Perhaps the greatest problems were those of unifying the State politically and of making a constitution work.[65]

Major Battles of the Revolutionary War

Quebec
Dec. 31, 1775

Nova Scotia

Montreal
Nov. 13, 1775

Maine
(Part of Mass.)

Crown Point

Ft. Ticonderoga

New Hampshire

Saratoga
Oct. 17, 1777

Concord (Apr. 19, 1775)
Lexington (Apr. 19, 1775)
Bunker Hill (June 17, 1775)

L. Ontario

Oriskany
Aug. 6, 1777

Bennington
Aug. 16, 1777

Massachusetts

New York

Rhode Island

White Plains

Connecticut

L. Erie

Pennsylvania

Germantown
Oct. 4, 1777

Long Island (Aug. 27, 1776)
Princeton (Jan. 3, 1777)
Monmouth (June 28, 1778)
Trenton (Dec. 26, 1776)

Brandywine
Sep. 11, 1777

New Jersey

Delaware

Maryland

Virginia

Yorktown
Oct. 6-19, 1781

ATLANTIC OCEAN

Great Bridge
Dec. 9, 1775

Guilford Court House
March 15, 1781

King's Mountain
Oct. 7, 1780

North Carolina

Moore's Creek Bridge
Feb. 27, 1776

[Hannah's] Cowpens
Jan. 17, 1781

Camden
Aug. 16, 1780

South
Carolina

Charleston
May 12, 1780

Georgia

Savannah
Dec. 29, 1778

Another of the new government's most pressing problems was recruiting and training soldiers for the Revolution. In the summer of 1776, North Carolina sent fourteen hundred troops to help defend Charleston against the British and raised an army of twenty-four hundred soldiers to combat the Cherokee, who they feared would join the British and attack in western counties. The Cherokee were subdued and the British attempt to control the South early in the war failed.

But in December 1779, a huge fleet of more than a hundred troop carriers left New York Harbor bound for Charleston, where Lord Charles Cornwallis began a final British drive to conquer southern states. North Carolina would become a key battleground in this phase of the war.

British Invasion

After capturing Charleston on May 12, 1780, following a long and bloody siege, Cornwallis wanted to pacify the rest of South Carolina, defeat the patriots in North Carolina, and then advance into Virginia. British troops in August scored a victory at Camden, South Carolina, against a large American force led by Major General Horatio Gates, who fled the field in disgrace, and they soon controlled South Carolina. Cornwallis seemed unstoppable, and his next target was North Carolina.

But the British received an angry welcome when they crossed the border into North Carolina. Patriots attacked Cornwallis and his troops from all sides, slowing down their advance so much that it took them seventeen days to travel seventy miles from Camden to Charlotte. It was in North Carolina, which Cornwallis termed the "hornet's nest of the revolution,"[66] that the tide of war would turn irrevocably in favor of the Americans.

King's Mountain

The British invaded the South because they incorrectly believed it was home to thousands of Loyalists who would help them win the war. Although there were far fewer Loyalists than the British had thought, Cornwallis assembled a large Loyalist force led by Major Patrick Ferguson, a Scot who entered North Carolina in a bid to

Armed with flintlock rifles and tomahawks, frontier colonists defeated Patrick Ferguson and his band of Loyalists in the Battle of King's Mountain.

defeat local militia and recruit more Loyalists. When militia and volunteer soldiers began to fight back, Ferguson positioned his force on King's Mountain, a stony, flat-topped ridge with steep sides near the South Carolina border. He then foolishly boasted, "I am on King's Mountain. I am king of the mountain and God Almighty will not drive me from it."[67]

Ferguson, however, had underestimated his pursuers. His brash challenge was answered by more than a thousand "over the mountain men," frontiersmen from west of the Appalachians, the area that would one day become Tennessee. Wearing buckskin shirts and coonskin hats and armed with flintlock rifles and tomahawks, they surrounded King's Mountain and on October 7 attacked, dashing up the hill into the withering fire from Ferguson's force of nine hundred.

Led by brave men like William Campbell, a Scot Patriot, the Americans were at first beaten back, but they kept charging and gradually overcame the British. Realizing he had lost, Ferguson tried to escape but was literally shot to pieces before he could ride away. Three hundred Loyalists died in a crushing defeat that historian Sir Henry Clinton, the overall commander of British troops, later called "the first link of a chain of evils that followed each other into regular succession until they at last ended in the total loss of America."[68]

Guilford Court House

In October General George Washington sent one of his top officers, Nathanael Greene, to stop the British. In January 1781 Greene's forces scored a major victory at Hannah's Cowpens, a meadow near Camden, South Carolina. At first Greene did not want to challenge Cornwallis's main force, so he led his men away into the wilderness. In March, however, Greene was ready to fight the British, and the result was the Battle of Guilford Court House, one of the bloodiest engagements of the Revolutionary War.

On March 16, Greene positioned his 4,400 men for battle at Guilford Court House, which was only a dozen miles from New Garden, where Cornwallis was camped. Greene placed local militia ahead of the Continentals, members of the regular U.S. Army, and

The Battle of Guilford Court House, one of the bloodiest battles of the Revolutionary War, was a costly victory for the British.

British soldiers relinquish their weapons to General George Washington. In October 1781, the British surrendered to the colonists.

waited for Cornwallis to attack. The British had a smaller force of 2,253, but they were battle-hardened veterans. In the fierce fighting that followed the opening charges by the two armies, the British suffered 93 dead and 439 wounded while Greene's casualties totaled 1,255; most of Greene's men, however, were declared "missing in action" and later returned.

The British drove the Americans from the field but at so great a cost—almost 25 percent of their men had been killed or wounded—that Charles James Fox, a member of the British House of Commons, commented, "Another such victory would ruin the British army."[69] Even Cornwallis, who had experienced many bloody battles himself, admitted, "I never saw such fighting since God made me. The Americans fought like demons."[70]

Victory at Yorktown

After this setback in North Carolina, Cornwallis shifted his attention to Virginia, where he hoped to defeat the Patriots in a series of strategic battles. After unsuccessfully trying to capture American forces led by the Marquis de Lafayette, Cornwallis went to Richmond and then Yorktown, a port city where he expected the

British fleet to arrive and help him. Instead, an army commanded by Washington surrounded him and on September 7 began a siege that lasted until October 19, when Cornwallis surrendered. On that day the British marched out of Yorktown with their band playing the tune "The World Turned Upside Down."

The world, indeed, had turned topsy-turvy. America had won the Revolutionary War. North Carolina was no longer a British colony, but a free and independent state.

Chapter Five

North Carolina: Learning to Live in Freedom

O nce North Carolina and the other colonies had won their freedom in the Revolutionary War, they had to learn how to govern themselves. In an April 19, 1783, address to the General Assembly, North Carolina governor Alexander Martin prophesied that this would be an easy task: "Nothing now remains but to enjoy the fruits of uninterrupted Constitutional freedom."[71] But Frederick William Marschall of Salem provided a more accurate assessment of the situation that confronted his nation and state:

> This country is in the condition of a patient convalescing from a fever, who begins to become conscious of his weakness and still needs medicine and care. The land itself, the people of property, commerce, public and private credit, the currency in circulation all are laid waste and ruined.[72]

The period from the end of the Revolutionary War to the adoption of the Constitution in 1789 was difficult for people in North Carolina and the other twelve former colonies that had banded together to become the United States of America. The 350,000 people living in North Carolina's forty-seven counties faced a wide variety of complex problems: weak and inefficient government, political divisions on how the state and nation should be governed, and a shattered economy.

One of the most difficult challenges was how to heal lingering resentments against Loyalists who opposed the fight for independence. It was a task made much more difficult by violence that occurred after the British left North Carolina near the end of the Revolutionary War.

Forgiving Loyalists

In April 1781 when Lord Charles Cornwallis set out for Virginia and the climactic battles of the war, Loyalist and British soldiers accompanying him plundered farms and plantations along their route. It was the start of the Tory War, a bloody struggle between Loyalists and Whigs that continued even after the Revolution had been won and that created a great deal of hatred, as historian William S. Powell explains:

> The departure of the [American and British] armies left North Carolina at the mercy of many loosely organized, undisciplined bands of armed men, Patriot and Loyalist alike. For more than a year they carried on a relentless civil war, and the state was the victim of pillage, murder, and general disorder. These events largely explain the bitterness many people felt toward the Loyalists [after the war], most of whom lived in the Cape Fear River Valley.[73]

During the Revolution, the Patriots controlled North Carolina government. Some Loyalists left the state to fight for the British, and those who remained in the former colony tried to undermine the Patriot cause: They refused to cooperate with state officials,

Lord Charles Cornwallis and his troops plundered farms and plantations in North Carolina on their way to Virginia near the end of the war.

tried to stop formation of local militias, and even engaged in military-style raids, destroying property and killing Patriots. Emboldened by the British invasion of North Carolina, Loyalists continued to fight after Cornwallis left.

The Tory War pitted undisciplined groups of armed men on both sides in a final battle for control of North Carolina, some of them criminals whose sole aim was to loot and destroy property. The most infamous Tory was David Fanning, a Loyalist colonel reviled for indiscriminately killing women and children in his attacks. His most famous raid was on September 12, 1781, when he routed local militia in Hillsborough and captured Governor Thomas Burke, who he turned over to British authorities. Although the last British troops left North Carolina in October 1781, Fanning continued raiding rural areas until the following May, when he fled to Canada to end the Tory War.

In 1783 the state had passed an Act of Pardon and Oblivion to forgive Loyalists for their actions during the war, but it failed to exonerate many who fought for the British and did little to bring the two sides together. During the Revolutionary War, the state had also approved Confiscation Acts that empowered it to seize Loyalist property and sell it to support the Revolution. The Treaty of Paris that ended the war recommended returning such confiscated property, but North Carolinians were not as charitable. Most Loyalists never got their land or homes back, a situation that even many Patriots realized was unjust. William Hooper, for one, claimed that many of the seizures were made by people who used the war to steal property: "There is not a frenzy of misguided political zeal—avarice clothed in the cover of patriotism—of private passion and prejudice, under the pretence of revenging the wrongs of the country that can give me the least surprise hereafter."[74]

It would take many years for North Carolinians to forgive neighbors and even members of their own family who had opposed independence, and many Loyalists were treated so harshly that hundreds moved to England, Canada, and other British possessions. But as these Loyalists were leaving North Carolina, hundreds of soldiers who had been held prisoner by the British were returning home.

A Weak Economy

Thousands of North Carolinians fought in the Revolution with the Continental army and state and local militia units, and hundreds became prisoners of war. At least 815 Continental and 700 militia soldiers were captured when Charleston fell to the British on May 12, 1780, and General Griffith Rutherford and hundreds of other state soldiers were taken prisoner after the Battle of Camden on August 16, 1780.

A top priority for officials was getting those prisoners home, which they did immediately, and then rewarding all state soldiers who fought for freedom. During the Revolution, North Carolina had often been unable to pay soldiers because of a lack of funds, and the state's treasury was still depleted after it won its freedom. So North Carolina gave war veterans the only thing of value it had, tracts of land west of the Appalachian range. These bonuses ranged from 640 acres for a private up to 12,000 acres for a brigadier general.

North Carolina and other states were deep in debt after the war because it cost so much to fight the British. North Carolina's postwar financial problems were compounded by an economic slump due to the loss of its main trading partner—Great Britain—and the general disruption of commerce with other states. Historian Powell explains:

> Paper money became virtually worthless and there was little profit in agriculture [the industry most North Carolinians were involved in] that produced more than was needed for home consumption. Commerce all but stopped. Hundreds of families were reduced from ease and comfort to poverty and misery.[75]

Gradually, however, the state economy revived. North Carolina began to sell other nations tobacco, naval stores, and other products, and it profited from the sale of land to new settlers.

A Weak Government

In addition to a weakened economy, North Carolina after the war suffered from political strife as legislators and other officials split into two opposing groups. Historians Hugh Talmadge Lefler and Albert Ray Newsome explain this division:

> Party politics in the state from 1781 to 1789 was characterized by personal factionalism and sectional interests. There were two major groups—Conservatives and Radicals, a division that bore a close relation to social classes, economic interests, and geography. The Conservatives embraced lawyers, merchants, shippers, large planters and slaveholders, land speculators, and moneylenders. Most of the educated, the wealthy, and the creditor class were in this "party," which constituted a small minority of the population. The Radicals constituted the great bulk of North Carolina people—small farmers and artisans—many of them uneducated, poor, and in debt.[76]

The radicals, most of whom were in debt to North Carolina or British lenders, demanded more paper money (a move that would ease their debt repayment), further confiscation of Loyalist property, and erasure of all debts to Great Britain. The conservatives held the opposite view on every issue. The political animosity weakened state government because lawmakers and other officials continually disagreed. Powell notes that for many years following independence, "political questions were resolved chiefly in terms of sectional, local, and personal interests, and political activities [remained] intense and bitter."[77]

One of the most divisive issues was where to establish a permanent capital. Because New Bern had been vulnerable to British attack when the Revolution began, the state in 1777 reverted to an earlier tradition of moving legislative sessions from town to town, a practice that created confusion and inefficiency in government. In 1792 the state realized it needed to establish a permanent seat of government, but a fierce political battle arose as many cities fought to be chosen as the new capital.

The State House at North Carolina's capital city, Raleigh was created as a solution to the political struggle over the location of the state capital.

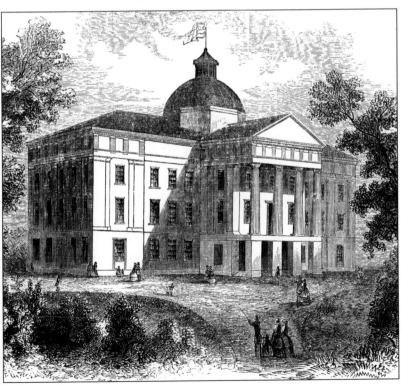

North Carolina eventually decided the best solution was to create a new city. It bought a thousand acres of land from plantation owner Joel Lane and named the new capital after Sir Walter Raleigh. Although critics claimed the new site "would never rise above the degree of a village,"[78] Raleigh quickly became one of North Carolina's most important communities.

This political division that hampered the efficiency of state government also created a major problem in North Carolina's relationship with the new federal government of the United States.

Mistrust of Government Power

North Carolina's experience with proprietary and royal governors who governed them poorly had left state residents with a distrust of a strong central government. The other colonies shared this distrust, which was reflected in the Articles of Confederation, written during the American Revolution to establish how the federal government would operate. The North Carolina delegates who helped draft the Articles—Cornelius Harnett, John Penn, and Thomas Burke—had all sought to protect the rights of individual states by keeping the central government weak. Burke demanded that "each state retain its sovereignty, freedom and independence," and Harnett, in a letter to Burke, once wrote, "I fear it [the Confederation] will by several Legislatures be thought a little Deformed; you will think it a Monster."[79] Despite their misgivings, the North Carolina General Assembly approved the Articles of Confederation on April 24, 1778.

After the Revolution, however, it became apparent that the Articles had created a system so weak that it could not adequately govern the nation, and the U.S. Constitution was drafted to establish a better system. In North Carolina, with its traditional opposition to a strong central government, there was so much resistance to the Constitution, that for a while it looked like the state would never approve it.

Constitutional Battle

A Constitutional Convention was convened in Philadelphia in May 1787 after the states realized their current form of government had failed. Delegates from North Carolina were Alexander Martin, Richard Dobbs Spaight, William R. Davie, Hugh Williams, and William Blount. The delegation agreed that the federal government needed more power than the Articles of Confederation gave it, but not so much as to endanger North Carolina's rights.

After the Constitution was finally drafted in September after four grueling months of debate, a fierce political fight developed in North Carolina and other states on whether it should be accepted. Those backing it were known as Federalists and those opposing it were called Antifederalists; in North Carolina the Federalists were mainly people who had previously been labeled conservatives, and the Antifederalists came from the ranks of the radicals. The undisputed North Carolina Antifederalist leader was Willie Jones of Halifax County. Historian John C. Cavanagh explains why Jones opposed the Constitution:

A R T I C L E S

O F

Confederation

A N D

Perpetual Union

BETWEEN THE *S.H.M.*

S   T   A   T   E   S

O F

NEW-HAMPSHIRE, MASSACHUSETTS-BAY, RHODE-ISLAND AND PROVIDENCE PLANTATIONS, CONNECTICUT, NEW-YORK, NEW-JERSEY, PENNSYLVANIA, DELAWARE, MARYLAND, VIRGINIA, NORTH-CAROLINA, SOUTH-CAROLINA AND GEORGIA.

L A N C A S T E R:
PRINTED BY F R A N C I S B A I L E Y.
M,DCC,LXXVII.

The North Carolina delegates who helped draft the Articles of Confederation sought to protect the rights of individual states, having developed a distrust for strong central government.

Jones and his [supporters] held genuine misgivings that the federal Constitution, unless carefully amended, did not properly guarantee the rights and liberties that North Carolinians enjoyed under their own state bill of rights. Jones prided his state on its virtually independent self-sufficiency and for operating under a more genuinely

87

George Washington presiding over the 1787 Constitutional Convention. Despite North Carolina's rejection of the document, the Constitution went into effect June 21, 1788.

democratic administration than he suspected could survive under a strong federal union.[80]

North Carolina held a convention in Hillsborough in July 1788 to vote on the Constitution. The delegates were overwhelmingly Antifederalist and refused to approve the document, although they did not give it an outright rejection. With a vote of 184 to 84, delegates passed a resolution saying that North Carolina would not approve the document until a "declaration of rights" was added to protect "the great Principles of civil and religious Liberty, and the unalienable rights of the People."[81]

The result was that North Carolina helped prod national officials into drafting a bill of rights, the guarantee of individual freedom the Antifederalists wanted. The Hillsborough Convention passed its own Declaration of Rights, twenty in all, and presented them to Congress, which used them along with suggestions from other states to create the Bill of Rights.

Despite North Carolina's refusal to approve the Constitution, it went into effect June 21, 1788, after New Hampshire became the ninth state to ratify it, and by July 1788 only North Carolina and Rhode Island had failed to accept it. A second ratification convention was scheduled in Fayetteville for November 1789, by which time the new federal government was already operating. Because their state failed to accept the Constitution, North Carolinians were not allowed to vote in the first presidential election, which was won by George Washington, and were not represented in the first session of Congress.

Washington, mindful of the need to unify the nation, sent a conciliatory message to delegates attending the second ratification convention, pronouncing a "Divine benediction [on] the councils which are shortly to [decide] the political relation between the State of North Carolina and the States now in Union."[82] The president's

Painting of George Washington by Charles Wilson Peale. North Carolina could not participate in the election in which Washington became president because they had failed to ratify the Constitution.

blessing may not have won any votes for ratification, but the promise of a bill of rights and the growing realization that acceptance was inevitable helped shift public opinion toward the Federalist viewpoint, and on November 21 delegates approved the Constitution 195 to 77 (Rhode Island would not ratify it until May 1790).

New Settlement

One of the postwar disagreements North Carolina and other states had with the federal government was its demand that they surrender

North Carolina's Declaration of Rights

North Carolina's constitutional delegates declared they would not accept the Constitution unless it included a list of basic rights that citizens would be guaranteed. The delegates sent Congress their own Declaration of Rights. The following excerpts from that declaration are from The North Carolina Experience: An Interpretive and Documentary History *by Lindley S. Butler and Alan D. Watson:*

1. That there are certain natural rights, of which men, when they form a social compact, cannot deprive or divest their posterity, among which are the enjoyment of life and liberty, with the means of acquiring, possession, and protecting property, and pursuing and obtaining happiness and safety.

2. That all power is naturally vested in, and consequently derived from, the people.

3. That government ought to be instituted for the common benefit, protection, and security of people...

5. That the legislative, executive, and judiciary powers of government should be separate and distinct.

6. That elections of representatives in the legislature ought to be free and frequent.

7. That all power of suspending law, or the execution of laws, by any authority, without the consent of the representatives of the

land bordering them; some states insisted their borders extended all
the way west to the Pacific Ocean. North Carolina claimed land only
to the Mississippi River, but the federal government was adamant
that it surrender this territory. The General Assembly in April 1784
passed a Cession Act to comply with that request, but within four
months conservatives won its repeal, claiming the area was too
valuable to give away.

The Cession Act inspired residents in land west of the mountains
to form an independent new state that they named Franklin after

people in the legislature, is injurious to their rights, and ought not
to be exercised.

8. That, in all capital and criminal prosecutions, a man hath a
right to demand the cause and nature of his accusation, to be
confronted with the accusers and witnesses, to call for evidence,
and be allowed counsel in his favor, and a fair and speedy trial by
an impartial jury of his [peers], without whose unanimous
consent he cannot be found guilty . . . nor can he be compelled to
give evidence against himself. . . .

15. That the people have a right peaceably to assemble together,
to consult for the common good, or to instruct representatives.

16. That the people have a right to freedom of speech, and of
writing and publishing their sentiments; that freedom of press is
one of the greatest bulwarks of liberty, and ought not to be violated.

17. That the people have a right to keep and bear arms; that a well-
regulated militia, composed of the body of the people, trained to
arms, is the property, natural, and safe defense of a free state.

18. That no soldier, in time of peace, ought to be quartered in any
house without the consent of the owner, and in time of war, in
such manner only as the laws direct.

20. [That]all men have an equal, natural, and unalienable right to
the free exercise of religion, according to the dictates of [their]
conscience; and that no particular religious sect or society ought
to be favored or established by law in preference to others.

Benjamin Franklin, one of the nation's founders. The effort to create a new state failed when North Carolina overturned the Cession Act, and North Carolina eventually gave land bordering it to the federal government when it ratified the Constitution. The ceded land included Washington, Davidson, Hawkins, Greene, Sullivan, Sumner, and Tennessee Counties, territory that in 1796 would become part of the state of Tennessee.

Not Everyone Benefits

North Carolina grew quickly after the Constitution was approved. In 1790 the state had 393,751 residents and was the third most populous state, ranking only behind Virginia and Pennsylvania, but by 1800 its population had swollen to 478,103. Thousands of new residents helped develop the entire state, but better times for whites did not mean better times for other North Carolinians—Indians, slaves, and free African Americans.

The influx of settlers into western North Carolina led to more clashes with Cherokee Indians, who were once again squeezed off their land. The Cherokee had remained peaceful since being subdued during the Revolution, but they were not rewarded for their good behavior. In 1785 and again in 1791, state and federal officials forced the tribe to sign new treaties that took away even more land. This pattern continued until the 1830s, when the remaining Cherokee were forced to move to Oklahoma Territory. Their journey became known as the Trail of Tears when thousands of them died along the way.

Another group who suffered were the 100,522 African American slaves, who in 1790 composed nearly a quarter of the state population, and 4,975 free African Americans. Neighboring states like Virginia and South Carolina had many more slaves in 1790, but the number of North Carolina slaves grew in the following years, and by 1820 there were over 205,000 slaves in the state. This increase was primarily due to the need for cheap labor to grow cotton, a product that became more profitable after the invention of the cotton gin. Historian H. G. Jones writes that life was difficult in North Carolina for African Americans:

> For blacks the Revolution changed little. As chattels, slaves were bought, sold, worked, punished, and furnished shelters

The State of Franklin

In 1784 a group of pioneers who settled in western North Carolina tried to create a new state. They named it Franklin after Benjamin Franklin, one of the most renowned of America's founders, but this proposed fourteenth state did not survive much longer than the Lost Colony on Roanoke Island two hundred years earlier. In North Carolina Through Four Centuries, *William Stevens Powell explains how the ill-fated state of Franklin was born out of North Carolina's decision to surrender western lands to the federal government:*

The cession act of April 1784 seemed to be virtually an invitation to form an independent government, and people beyond the mountains welcomed the prospect of being on an equal footing with their parent state. In August 1784 some citizens of Washington, Greene, and Sullivan Counties laid the foundations for a new state. In December the convention met in Jonesboro, after North Carolina had repealed the offer to cede the territory, and decided to pursue their dream in spite of the state's action. Delegates from all four counties were heartily in favor of creating the state of Franklin and adopted a constitution virtually identical to North Carolina. An early election was held, an assembly gathered, and in March 1785 John Sevier was chosen governor. Meanwhile Governor Alexander Martin of North Carolina dispatched an influential negotiator to the region, but the people rejected his overtures for a peaceful redirection of their loyalty to North Carolina. The residents of Franklin cited offensive names that their former legislature had called them— "offscourings of the earth" and "fugitives from Justice." Martin threatened to use force, though he probably was not certain that his militia would be willing to engage in battle with the sharpshooters across the mountains.

Powell explains that after the state of Franklin failed to win the approval of either Congress or its namesake, Benjamin Franklin, and the new state's government proved inefficient, the movement to create Franklin began to weaken and in 1788 collapsed entirely. The four counties were eventually combined with more territory and in 1796 became the state of Tennessee.

and sustenance, much as an owner would care for a work horse. The law, of course, differentiated between enslaved humans and other chattels, but a master's authority over his slave was seldom curtailed. Nor were the lives of the "free persons of colour" without great peril, for they carried no physical mark to distinguish them from blacks in bondage.[83]

In another half century, slavery would become the central issue that would lead North Carolina and other southern states to begin fighting in the Civil War. In 1790 the evil of slavery was something that was accepted in the state as an economic necessity.

Looking Forward

By 1800 North Carolinians had endured more than two centuries of often turbulent history. Despite the many problems they had encountered, historian Powell believes that residents of this southern state never gave up hope for a brighter future:

Slaves plant rice on a North Carolina plantation. Slavery would be the central issue to lead the state into civil war in the next half century.

North Carolinians, especially when the present was not particularly promising, have always looked to the future. The Roanoke colonists of the 1580s took a great risk in leaving England for a different kind of life in the New World wilderness, and as it turned out most of them paid with their lives. In the 1670s those who took matters into their own hands [to oppose the lords proprietors] obtained the reforms they sought and so did those who drew up the Halifax Resolves and who cast their lot with other revolutionists.[84]

It was this ability to encounter disaster, weather it, and then continue on that enabled settlers who ventured to North Carolina to transform it from a wilderness and to later battle the British for their independence to become one of the first thirteen members of the United States of America. It was this spirit that enabled them to make North Carolina a proud state.

Notes

Introduction: North Carolina: A Colony of Bewitching Beauty and Danger

1. Quoted in Hugh Talmadge Lefler and Albert Ray Newsome, *North Carolina: The History of a Southern State.* 3rd ed. Chapel Hill: University of North Carolina Press, 1973, p. 5.
2. Quoted in H. G. Jones, ed., *North Carolina Illustrated: 1524–1984.* Chapel Hill: University of North Carolina Press, 1983, p. 23.
3. Quoted in Blackwell P. Robinson, ed., *The North Carolina Guide.* Chapel Hill: University of North Carolina Press, 1955, p. 13.
4. Quoted in Lindley S. Butler and Alan D. Watson, *The North Carolina Experience: An Interpretive and Documentary History.* Chapel Hill: University of North Carolina Press, 1984, p. 93.
5. Quoted in Butler and Watson, *The North Carolina Experience,* p. 93.
6. Lefler and Newsome, *North Carolina,* p. 30.
7. William B. Hesseltine, *A History of the South.* New York: Prentice-Hall, 1938, p. 70.

Chapter One: North Carolina's Difficult Beginning

8. William S. Powell, *North Carolina: A Bicentennial History.* New York: W. W. Norton, 1976, p. 21.
9. Powell, *North Carolina,* p. 11.
10. Paul Johnson, *A History of the American People.* New York: HarperCollins, 1997, p. 12.
11. Quoted in Robinson, *The North Carolina Guide,* p. 13.
12. Quoted in Butler and Watson, *The North Carolina Experience,* p. 40.
13. Quoted in Johnson, *A History of the American People,* p. 16.
14. Quoted in Johnson, *A History of the American People,* p. 17.
15. Quoted in Jones, *North Carolina Illustrated,* p. 5.
16. Quoted in William Stevens Powell, *North Carolina Through*

Four Centuries. Chapel Hill: University of North Carolina Press, 1989, p. 48.

17. David Stick, *Roanoke Island: The Beginnings of English America.* Chapel Hill: University of North Carolina Press, 1983, p. 216.
18. Quoted in Lefler and Newsome, *North Carolina*, p. 5.
19. Quoted in Hugh T. Lefler and William S. Powell, *Colonial North Carolina: A History.* New York: Charles Scribner's Sons, 1973, p. 2.
20. Quoted in Butler and Watson, *The North Carolina Experience*, p. 14.
21. Quoted in Lefler and Newsome, *North Carolina*, p. 9.
22. Quoted in Michael Kraus, *The United States to 1865.* Ann Arbor: University of Michigan Press, 1969, p. 32.

Chapter Two: The Colony Struggles to Grow
23. Lefler and Newsome, *North Carolina*, p. 19.
24. Quoted in Lefler and Powell, *Colonial North Carolina*, p. 48.
25. Louis B. Wright, *The Atlantic Frontier: Colonial American Civilization [1607–1763].* Ithaca, NY: Cornell University Press, 1947, p. 45.
26. Quoted in Lefler and Powell, *Colonial North Carolina*, p. 64.
27. Quoted in Joanne Young, *North Carolina: The First Two Hundred Years.* Birmingham, AL: Oxmoor House, 1975, p. 31.
28. Quoted in Butler and Watson, *The North Carolina Experience*, p. 17.
29. Quoted in Robert E. Lee, *Blackbeard the Pirate: A Reappraisal of His Life and Times.* Charlotte, NC: Heritage Printers, 1976, p. 20.
30. Robinson, *The North Carolina Guide*, p. 55.
31. Wright, *The Atlantic Frontier*, p. 280.
32. Johnson, *A History of the American People*, p. 897.
33. Lefler and Powell, *Colonial North Carolina*, p. 113.
34. Quoted in Robinson, *The North Carolina Guide*, p. 59.
35. Quoted in Lefler and Newsome, *North Carolina*, p. 78.
36. Quoted in Lefler and Newsome, *North Carolina*, p. 186.
37. Quoted in Butler and Watson, *The North Carolina Experience*, p. 106.

Chapter Three: Life in Colonial North Carolina

38. Quoted in Robinson, *The North Carolina Guide,* p. 13.
39. Quoted in Patricia Hudson and Sandra L. Ballard, *The Smithstonian Guides to Historic America: The Carolinas and the Appalachian States.* New York: Stewart, Tabori & Chang, 1998, p. 22.
40. Jones, *North Carolina Illustrated,* p. 209.
41. Quoted in Lefler and Newsome, *North Carolina,* p. 23.
42. Lefler and Powell, *Colonial North Carolina,* p. 175.
43. Quoted in Lefler and Newsome, *North Carolina,* p. 93.
44. Hesseltine, *A History of the South,* p. 76.
45. Quoted in Jones, *North Carolina Illustrated,* p. 54.
46. Quoted in Oliver Perry Chitwood, *A History of Colonial America.* 3rd ed. New York: Harper & Row, 1961, p. 197.
47. Quoted in Powell, *North Carolina,* p. 46.
48. Quoted in Robinson, *The North Carolina Guide,* p. 65.
49. Quoted in Jones, *North Carolina Illustrated,* p. 54.
50. Robinson, *The North Carolina Guide,* p. 60.
51. Quoted in Young, *North Carolina,* p. 50.
52. Young, *North Carolina,* p. 80.

Chapter Four: North Carolina in the Revolutionary War

53. Johnson, *A History of the American People,* p. 89.
54. Lefler and Newsome, *North Carolina,* p. 231.
55. Jeffrey J. Crow, *A Chronicle of North Carolina During the American Revolution 1768–1789.* Raleigh: North Carolina Division of Archives and History, 1997, p. 9.
56. Quoted in Young, *North Carolina,* p. 86.
57. Quoted in Powell, *North Carolina Through Four Centuries,* p. 160.
58. Quoted in Young, *North Carolina,* p. 98.
59. Quoted in Lefler and Powell, *Colonial North Carolina,* p. 268.
60. Powell, *North Carolina,* p. 39.
61. Quoted in Young, *North Carolina,* p. 101.
62. Crow, *A Chronicle of North Carolina,* p. 27.
63. Quoted in *North Carolina Encyclopedia,* www.statelibrary.dcr.state.nc.us/nc/history/history.html.
64. Quoted in Robert L. Ganyard, *The Emergence of North*

Carolina's Revolutionary State Government. Raleigh: North
Carolina Division of Archives and History, 1978, p. 85.

65. Robinson, *The North Carolina Guide,* p. 70.
66. Quoted in Powell, *North Carolina,* p. 71.
67. Quoted in John Selby, *The Road to Yorktown.* New York: St.
    Martin's Press, 1976, p. 175.
68. Quoted in Page Smith, *A New Age Now Begins: A People's
    History of the American Revolution.* Vol. 2. New York: McGraw-
    Hill, 1976, p. 1,443.
69. Quoted in Smith, *A New Age Now Begins,* p. 1,484.
70. Quoted in Lefler and Newsome, *North Carolina,* p. 252.

Chapter Five: North Carolina: Learning to Live in Freedom
71. Quoted in Young, *North Carolina,* p. 134.
72. Quoted in Jones, *North Carolina Illustrated,* p. 133.
73. Powell, *North Carolina,* p. 78.
74. Quoted in Lefler and Newsome, *North Carolina,* p. 257.
75. Powell, *North Carolina Through Four Centuries,* p. 209.
76. Lefler and Newsome, *North Carolina,* pp. 255–56.
77. Powell, *North Carolina Through Four Centuries,* p. 192.
78. Quoted in Butler and Watson, *The North Carolina Experience,*
    p. 149.
79. Quoted in John C. Cavanagh, *Decision at Fayetteville: The
    North Carolina Ratification Convention and General Assembly of
    1789.* Raleigh: North Carolina Division of Archives and
    History, 1989, p. 15.
80. Cavanagh, *Decision at Fayetteville,* p. 17.
81. Quoted in Jones, *North Carolina Illustrated,* p. 134.
82. Quoted in Cavanaugh, *Decision at Fayetteville,* p. 17.
83. Quoted in Jones, *North Carolina Illustrated,* p. 136.
84. Powell, *North Carolina Through Four Centuries,* p. 553.

Chronology

1524

In March, Giovanni da Verrazano explores for France along what is now the North Carolina coast.

1526

In July, Spanish explorer Lucas Vázquez de Ayllón tries to start a colony along the Cape Fear River, but it is abandoned by October.

1584

On March 25, Queen Elizabeth grants Sir Walter Raleigh the right to settle land in the New World; on July 13, an expedition dispatched by Raleigh lands on the North Carolina coast and claims it for England.

1585

On January 6, Queen Elizabeth knights Raleigh and grants him permission to name land in the New World after her—Virginia; on July 21, the colony led by Sir Richard Grenville and Ralph Lane reaches Roanoke Island.

1586

On June 10, British explorer Sir Francis Drake arrives at Roanoke Island to check on the Lane colony; a week later, Lane and his remaining men sail back to England with Drake.

1587

On July 22, a group of colonists led by John White return to Roanoke Island; on August 18, Virginia Dare is the first English child born in the New World.

1590

On August 17, three years after he returned to England for more supplies, John White returns to Roanoke Island to discover that the 107 people he left behind have disappeared. They become known as the "Lost Colony."

1663

On March 24, Charles II grants Carolana, a large area that included

North Carolina, to eight of his supporters who become known as the lords proprietors.

1710

New Bern is founded at the junction of the Trent and Neuse Rivers by Baron Christoph von Graffenried, a leader of Swiss and German Protestants.

1711

On September 22, the Tuscarora War begins when the Tuscarora and several other tribes attack colonial settlements, killing more than 130 whites; fighting continues periodically until 1715.

1712

On May 12, the lords proprietors officially divide their grant into North Carolina and South Carolina.

1718

On November 22, British lieutenant Robert Maynard kills Edward Teach, the pirate known as Blackbeard.

1729

On July 25, North Carolina becomes a royal colony when King George II purchases shares from seven of the eight lords proprietors; only the earl of Granville refuses to sell.

1751

In August, James Davis begins publishing the *North Carolina Gazette*, the colony's first newspaper, in New Bern.

1753

On November 17, the Moravians begin building the town of Bethabara.

1768

Farmers in Orange County organize the Regulators, a group that protests corrupt government officials.

1771

On May 16, in the Battle of Alamance, militia led by Governor William Tryon defeat the Regulators, ending the movement.

1774

On August 25–27, the First Provincial Congress meets in New Bern. It adopts resolutions criticizing acts and policies of the British government and elects three delegates to the First Continental

Congress; on October 25 at the Edenton Tea Party, fifty-one women resolve to support American independence.

1775

On April 19, the first battles of the American Revolution take place at Lexington and Concord (Massachusetts).

1776

On February 27, North Carolina Patriots defeat Highland Scots Loyalists at the Battle of Moore's Creek Bridge; on April 12, the Fourth Provincial Congress approves the Halifax Resolves, the first state call for independence; on December 18, the Provincial Congress adopts the first North Carolina state constitution and elects Richard Caswell governor.

1780

On May 12, the British capture Charleston, South Carolina; on October 7, Americans defeat Loyalists at the Battle of King's Mountain.

1781

On March 15, in the largest armed conflict in North Carolina during the war, the Battle of Guilford Court House results in a costly victory for British troops; on October 19, the British surrender at Yorktown, effectively ending fighting in the war.

1787

On September 17, William Blount, Richard Dobbs Spaight, and Hugh Williamson sign the U.S. Constitution for North Carolina.

1789

On November 21, North Carolina becomes the twelfth state to ratify the U.S. Constitution.

For Further Reading

H. G. Jones, ed., *North Carolina Illustrated: 1524–1984*. Chapel Hill: University of North Carolina Press, 1983. An interesting, well-documented book with more than 1,150 photos that help bring alive the history of this southern state.

Robert Kelley, *The Shaping of the American Past*. Vol. 1. Englewood Cliffs, NJ: Prentice Hall, 1990. A solid reference work on American history that explains why things happened as well as what happened.

William S. Powell, *North Carolina: A Bicentennial History*. New York: W. W. Norton, 1976. An excellent history by one of the foremost North Carolina scholars.

David Stick, *Roanoke Island: The Beginnings of English America*. Chapel Hill: University of North Carolina Press, 1983. A scholarly look at the first English attempts to colonize the New World.

Joanne Young, *North Carolina: The First Two Hundred Years*. Birmingham, AL: Oxmoor House, 1975. A readable history that incudes many good pictures that complement the text.

Works Consulted

Books

Lindley S. Butler and Alan D. Watson, *The North Carolina Experience: An Interpretive and Documentary History*. Chapel Hill: University of North Carolina Press, 1984. The authors use historical documents to explain the state's history and intepret what happened.

John C. Cavanagh, *Decision at Fayetteville: The North Carolina Ratification Convention and General Assembly of 1789*. Raleigh: North Carolina Division of Archives and History, 1989. A detailed look at the con-vention that resulted in North Carolina's ratification of the U.S. Constitution.

Oliver Perry Chitwood, *A History of Colonial America*. 3rd ed. New York: Harper & Row, 1961. A solid book that details how the individual colonies evolved and eventually decided to fight for independence.

Jeffrey J. Crow, *A Chronicle of North Carolina During the American Revolution 1768–1789*. Raleigh: North Carolina Division of Archives and History, 1997. A good reference work that provides a detailed explanation of the history of this period.

Robert L. Ganyard, *The Emergence of North Carolina's Revolutionary State Government*. Raleigh: North Carolina Division of Archives and History, 1978. A scholarly reference work on how North Carolina state government evolved after the Revolution began.

William B. Hesseltine, *A History of the South*. New York: Prentice-Hall, 1938. An interesting interpretation of how southern colonies were established and developed as states.

Patricia Hudson and Sandra L. Ballard, *The Smithstonian Guides to Historic America: The Carolinas and the Appalachian States*. New York: Stewart, Tabori & Chang, 1998. Portions of this travel guide provide excellent sources of information on the history of North Carolina and some of its communities.

Paul Johnson, *A History of the American People*. New York: HarperCollins, 1997. A fine U.S. history that includes many insights into the events that shaped the nation.

Catherine Kozak and Mary Ellen Riddle, *The Insiders' Guide to North Carolina's Outer Banks*, 19th ed. Manteo, NC: Insiders' Publishing, 1998. A travel guide that includes solid historical details about this important area of North Carolina.

Michael Kraus, *The United States to 1865*. Ann Arbor: University of Michigan Press, 1969. The author explains the forces that shaped the nation through the Civil War.

Robert E. Lee, *Blackbeard the Pirate: A Reappraisal of His Life and Times*. Charlotte, NC: Heritage Printers, 1976. This book reviews Blackbeard's life and explains the historical context in which piracy developed and flourished.

Hugh Talmadge Lefler and Albert Ray Newsome, *North Carolina: The History of a Southern State*. 3rd ed. Chapel Hill: University of North Carolina Press, 1973. An encylopedic, ambitious work that is one of the most definitive histories of North Carolina.

Hugh T. Lefler and William S. Powell, *Colonial North Carolina: A History*. New York: Charles Scribner's Sons, 1973. A well-documented history of North Carolina up until the American Revolution began.

William S. Powell, *The Proprietors of Carolina*. Raleigh, NC: State Department of Archives and History, 1968. Brief individual biographies of the Lords Proprietors.

William Stevens Powell, *North Carolina Through Four Centuries*. Chapel Hill: University of North Carolina Press, 1989. One of the finest North Carolina historians does an excellent job of explaining the state's long history.

Blackwell P. Robinson, ed., *The North Carolina Guide*. Chapel Hill: University of North Carolina Press, 1955. This travel guide contains a brief but well-written and solidly researched history of North Carolina that is as good as any other its length ever written.

John Selby, *The Road to Yorktown*. New York: St. Martin's Press, 1976. This British military historian explains the military history of the Revolutionary War, including the North Carolina battles that helped decide the war's outcome.

Page Smith, *A New Age Now Begins: A People's History of the American Revolution*. Vol. 2. New York: McGraw-Hill, 1976. Volume 2 of one of the finest histories of the United States that has ever been written.

Louis B. Wright, *The Atlantic Frontier: Colonial American Civilization [1607–1763]*. Ithaca, NY: Cornell University Press, 1947. A scholarly work on how the original colonies were established and developed.

Internet Site
North Carolina Encyclopedia (www.statelibrary.dcr.state.nc.us/nc/history/history.html). A publication of the State Library of North Carolina that includes a detailed history of the state.

Index

Act of Pardon and Oblivion, 82

African Americans, 92

agriculture, 55

Albemarle, 42

Albemarle Sound, 14, 31–32

Amadas, Philip, 16, 23

American Husbandry (anonymous), 55

American Revolution. *See* Revolutionary War

Anglican Church, 59

Anson County, 47

Antifederalists, 87–88

Arcadia, 9

Articles of Confederation, 86–87

Atlantic Frontier: Colonial American Civilization [1607–1763], The (Wright), 40

Ballard, Sandra L., 35

Baptists, 59–60

Barker, Penelope, 68

Barker, Thomas, 68

Barlowe, Arthur, 16–18, 23

barrel staves, 55

Bath, 32, 39

Battle of Almance, 47

Battle of Camden, 83

Battle of Concord, 69

Battle of Guilford Court House, 77–78

Battle of Lexington, 69

Battle of Moore's Creek, 71, 73

Batts, Nathaniel, 31

beans, 55

Bear River Indians, 38

Berkeley, John Lord, 41

Berkeley, William, 41

Bethabara, 60–61

Bethlehem, 61

Bill of Rights, 88, 90

Blackbeard, 38–40

Blount, William, 87

Blue Ridge Mountains, 14

boards, 55

Bonnet, "Gentleman" Stede, 38

Boone, Daniel, 60

Boston, 67

Bricknell, John, 57, 59

Brief and True Report of the New Found Land of Virginia, A (Harriot), 20

Brunswick, 66

Burke, Thomas, 82, 86

Burrington, George, 44

Butler, Lindley S., 90

Byrd, William, II, 48–49

Camden, 77

Campbell, William, 76

Campbelltown, 59

Canada, 65, 83

canoe, 24

Cape Fear, 14–15, 70

Cape Fear River, 13, 59, 70

Cape Fear Valley, 44–45, 54, 59

Cape Hatteras, 14, 23

Cape Lookout, 14

Carolana, 28

Carteret, George, 41–42

Caswell, Richard, 69, 73

Cavanagh, John C., 87

Cession Act (1784), 91–92

Charles I, 28, 30, 41

Charles II, 28, 41

Charleston, 42, 75, 83

Charleston Harbor, 39

Charlotte, 45, 69

Chattoka, 35

Cherokee Indians, 25, 74–75, 92

Chesapeake Bay, 27

chickens, 55

Civil War, 94

Clinton, Henry, 77

Coastal Plain, 14

Colleton, John, 41
Colonial North Carolina (Lefler and Powell), 53
Committee of Safety, 69
Confiscation Acts, 82
Connor, R. D. W., 52, 58
conservatives, 84–85
Constitutional Convention, 86
Continental army, 83
Continental Congress, 67, 69, 71–72
Cooper, Anthony Ashley, 41
Coree Indians, 35, 37
corn, 55
Cornwallis, Charles, 75, 77–79, 81–82
counties, 51
cows, 55
Craven, William, 41
Croatoan, 21–22
Croatoan Indians, 23–24
Cromwell, Oliver, 41
Cross Creek, 59, 66
Crow, Jeffrey J., 66, 71
Cruizer (ship), 70

Dare, Ananias, 20
Dare, Eleanor, 20
Dare, Virginia, 21
Dare County, 14
Davidson County, 92
Davie, William R., 87
Davis, James, 56
de Ayllón, Lucas Vázquez, 13, 15
Declaration of Independence, 71, 90–91
Declaration of Rights, 88
Divers Voyages Touching the Discoverie of American and the Islands Adjacent (Hakluyt), 9
Dobbs, Arthur, 44, 69
Drake, Francis, 20

Eden, Charles, 39
Edenton Tea Party, 67–68
Edgecome County, 47
Elizabeth I (queen of England), 15–16, 18, 21, 36, 41
England, 36, 44, 55, 83

famine, 36
Fanning, David, 82

Fayetteville, 59, 89
Federalists, 87
Ferguson, Patrick, 75–76
Florida, 65
forests, 36
Forsyth County, 60
Fort Johnston, 70
Fort Raleigh, 18, 20–21
Fox, Charles James, 78
France, 65
Francis I, 9
Franklin, Benjamin, 92–93
Franklin (short-lived state), 91, 93

Gaelic language, 59
Gale, Christopher, 37
Gates, Horatio, 75
General Assembly, 72–73, 80, 86, 91
George II, 42, 48
Germans, 61–63, 70
Germany, 34, 44, 59
Gilbert, Henry, 15
Graffenried, Baron Christoph von, 34, 36
Great Almance Creek, 47
Great Britain
    Americans feel more resentment toward, 64–65
    colonization of North Carolina by, 15–18
    invades the South, 75–78
    North Carolina declares independence from, 67, 69, 72
    status of wealthy in, 53
    stops trading with North Carolina, 83–84
    taxation of colonies by, 65–67
    see also Revolutionary War
Greene, Nathanael, 77–78
Greene County, 92–93
Grenville, Richard, 18–20
Guilford Court House, 77–78

Hakluyt, Richard, 9
Halifax, 45, 71–72
Halifax Resolves, 71–73
Hannah's Cowpens, 77
Harnett, Cornelius, 86
Harriot, Thomas, 18, 20, 25
Harvey, John, 67
Hatteras Indians, 25
Hawkins County, 92

The Thirteen Colonies • North Carolina

headright system, 32
Heath, Robert, 28
Hesseltine, William B., 11, 34, 56
Hewes, Joseph, 69
hickory, 24
Highlanders, 59–61, 70–71
Hillsborough, 45, 47, 72, 88
Hillsborough Convention, 88
History of Carolina (Lawson), 9, 48
History of the American People, A (Paul
    Johnson), 15, 42, 64
History of the South, A (Hesseltine), 34, 56
hogs, 55
hominy, 24
Hooper, William, 69, 83
Hudson, Patricia, 35
Huguenots, 33–34
hurricane, 24
Hyde, Edward, 41
Hyde, Henry, 42

indentured servants, 34–35, 54
Indians
    conflicts between colonists and, 11,
        26–27, 74–75, 92
    Tuscarora War, 35–38
    first European encounters with, 23–27
    as slaves, 35, 54–55
Iredell, Arthur, 68
Iredell, James, 68
Ireland, 44, 60

James I, 27–28
Jamestown, 23–24, 27–28
Jefferson, Thomas, 57, 71
Johnson, Andrew, 61
Johnson, Charles, 39
Johnson, Paul, 15, 42, 64
Johnston, Gabriel, 44, 54
Johnston County, 47
Jones, H. G., 50, 92
Jones, Willie, 87
Jonesboro, 93

Kelley, Robert, 36
Kill Devil Hill, 14
kilts, 59
King, Elizabeth, 67–68
King's Mountain, 75–77

Kitty Hawk, 9
Kraus, Michael, 24

La Dauphine (ship), 8
Lafayette, Marquis de, 59, 78
Lake Mattamuskeet, 27
Lane, Joel, 86
Lane, Ralph, 18–20, 24, 27
Lawson, John, 9, 36–37, 48
Lefler, Hugh Talmadge
    on conflicts between Indians and
        colonists, 11
    on how Moravians established church-
        based communities, 60
    on North Carolina
        becoming a royal colony, 43–44
        division between Whigs and Tories in,
            65
        geography of, 14
        politics, after Revolutionary War, 84
        slow growth, 29
        social structure, 53
Little Scotland, 59
London, 36
lords proprietors, 40–42, 50–51
Lost Colony, 10, 20–23
Loyalists, 65, 70, 73, 75–76, 81–83
Lutherans, 59–61

Macdonald, Donald, 70–71
Machapunga Indians, 38
Manteo, 24
Marschall, Frederick William, 80
Martin, Alexander, 80, 87, 93
Martin, Josiah, 67, 69–70
Massachusetts, 69
Maynard, Robert M., 40
Mecklenburg Declaration of
    Independence, 69
Meherrin Indians, 35
Methodists, 60
Mississippi River, 91
Mississippi Valley, 65
moccasin, 24
Monck, George, 41
Monticello, 57
Moore, "King" Roger, 54
Moore's Creek Bridge, 71
Moravians, 60–62, 70

Morning Chronicle (newspaper), 68

Native Americans. See Indians
Nettels, Curtis, 44
Neuse-Bern, 34
Neuse River, 32, 34, 37
New Bern, 34–35, 45–46, 66, 69–70, 73–74
New Hampshire, 88
Newsome, Albert Ray
  on conflicts between Indians and
  colonists, 11
  on how Moravians established church-
  based communities, 60
  on North Carolina
  divisions between Whigs and Tories in,
  65
  geography of, 14
  politics of, after Revolutionary War, 84
  slow growth of, 29
New York Harbor, 75
North Carolina
  becomes a state, 71–75
  colonization of
  arrival of
    Germans, 61–63
    Scottish Highlanders, 59–61
  becomes royal colony, 42–44
  by de Ayllón, 13, 15
  by Great Britain, 15–28
  conflicts between Indians and settlers
    in, 11, 26–27, 35–38
  first settlers in, 31–35
  government of, 50–51
  growth of, 29–30, 40, 44–46
  independent spirit of colonists in, 63
  mismanagement of, by lords
    proprietors, 40–42
  Regulators try to reform government
    of, 46–47
  threats from pirates in, 38–40
  disputes over U.S. Constitution in, 87–90
  early descriptions of, 9
  economy of, 55–56, 83–84
  geography of, 14
  government problems in, 84–86
  life in
    class distinctions in, 53–55
    culture in, 56–59
    early days of colonists in, 50–53
  ease of living in, 48–49
  population of, 92
  Revolutionary War and
    British invasion of, 75
    conflicts between Whigs and Tories in,
    65
    declares independence from Great
    Britain, 67, 69, 72
    Edenton Tea Party, 67–68
    effects of Tory War on, 81–83
    Patriots take control of, 70–71
    protests passage of Stamp Act, 65–66
  slavery in, 92, 94
  U.S. government demands surrender of
    bordering land, 90–92
North Carolina: A Bicentennial History
  (Powell), 24
*North Carolina: The First Two Hundred
  Years* (Young), 68
*North Carolina: The History of a Southern
  State* (Lefler and Newsome), 11, 14, 60
North Carolina Assembly, 67, 69
North Carolina Encyclopedia (State
  Library of North Carolina), 50
*North Carolina Experience: An Interpretive
  and Documentary History, The* (Butler
  and Watson), 90
North Carolina Gazette (newspaper), 56
North Carolina Through Four Centuries
  (Powell), 93
Northern Ireland, 59

Ocracoke Island, 40
Oklahoma Territory, 92
opossum, 24
Orange County, 47
Outer Banks, 17, 29, 38

Pacific Ocean, 91
Pamlico Indians, 37
Pamlico River, 32, 37
Pamlico Sound, 14
Patriots, 65, 70–71, 75–76, 81–83
peas, 55
Penn, John, 86
Pennsylvania, 30, 60–61
persimmon, 24
Philadelphia, 67, 86

Piedmont, 61
Piedmont Plain, 14
pirates, 30, 39–40
pitch, 55
plantations, 57
planter class, 54
Plymouth, 24
Polk, James, 61
Powell, William Stevens
  on birth of the state of Franklin, 93
  on Indians helping colonists at Roanoke
    Island, 24
  on lords proprietors, 41
  on North Carolina
    becoming a royal colony, 43–44
    economy of, after Revolutionary War, 84
    first settlements, 15
    future of, 94–95
    politics in, after Revolutionary War,
      85
    social structure, 53
  on Scotch support of British, 70
  on Tory War, 81
Powhatan, 23
Powhatan River, 27
precincts, 51
Presbyterians, 59–60
printing press, 56
Provincial Congress
  First, 67–69
  Fourth, 71–72
  Fifth, 71

Quakers, 59, 70
Quinn, David B., 27
quitrent, 32

raccoon, 24
radicals, 84
Raleigh, 86
Raleigh, Walter, 15–18, 20, 27, 29, 55
Ralph Lane Colony, 18–20
Reformed, 60–61
Regulators, 46–47
Revolutionary War
  battle at King's Mountain, 75–77
  Battle of Guilford Court House, 77–78
  beginning of, 69
  Great Britain and

invasion of the south by, 75
surrenders at Yorktown, 79
Patriots take control of North Carolina,
  70–71
Tory War, 81–83
Rhode Island, 88, 90
rice, 55
Richmond, 78
Roanoke Indians, 23
Roanoke Island, 10, 16–24, 27, 29
Roanoke Island: The Beginnings of English
  America (Stick), 22–23
Roanoke River, 32
Robinson, Blackwell P., 40, 61, 73
rosin, 56
Rutherford, Griffith, 83

Salem, 45
  see also Winston-Salem
Salisbury, 44–45
Schaw, Janet, 58
Scotch Irish, 59–61, 70
Scotland, 44, 59
Scots, 59–61, 70–71
Secotal Indians, 27
Shaping of the American Past, The
  (Kelley), 36
shingles, 55
slaves, 34–35, 54–55, 92
Smithsonian Guides to Historic America:
  The Carolinas and the Appalachian
  States, The (Hudson and Ballard), 35
Sons of Liberty, 66
Sothel, Seth, 42
South Carolina, 18, 30, 44–45, 57, 75–77
South Seas, 28
Southern Appalachians, 14
Spaight, Richard Dobbs, 87
Spain, 65
Spangenberg, August Gottlieb, 60–62
Stamp Act, 65–67
State Library of North Carolina, 50, 72
Stick, David, 23
Stuarts, 41
sugar, 65
Sullivan County, 92–93
Sumner County, 92
Switzerland, 34

tar, 55
Teach, Edward. *See* Blackbeard
Tennessee, 18, 92–93
Tennessee County, 92
tobacco, 34–35, 55
tomahawk, 24
Tories. *See* Loyalists
Tory War, 81–83
Trail of Tears, 92
Treaty of Paris, 82
Trent River, 34
Tryon, William, 46–47, 66
Tryon's Palace, 46
turpentine, 55
Tuscarora Indians, 25, 35–38

United Brethren. *See* Moravians
United States to 1865, The (Kraus), 24
U.S. Constitution, 86–90, 92

Verrazano, Giovanni da, 8–9, 23
Virginia
  becomes envious of life in North
    Carolina, 48
  borders North Carolina colony, 32
  British surrender in Yorktown, 78–79
  colonists move to North Carolina from,
    30–31, 50
  culture in, 57
  declares independence from Great
    Britain, 71

friendliness of Indians in, 24
indentured servants and slaves in, 34
number of colonists in Jamestown, 28
origin of, 18
road extended across North Carolina to,
  44
views of North Carolinians, 58
Virginia Company of London, 27–28
Virgin Queen. *See* Elizabeth I

Wachovia, 61
Wagoner, Hans, 60
Wales, 44
Wanchese, 23–24
Washington, George, 77, 89
Washington County, 92–93
Watson, Alan D., 90
wheat, 55
Wheeler, John H., 47
Whigs. *See* Patriots
White, John, 18, 20–23, 27
Williams, Edward, 9
Williams, Hugh, 87
Wilmington, 45, 58–59, 66, 70–71
Wingina, 27
Winston-Salem, 61
Wright, Louis B., 32, 40

Yamassee Indians, 38
Yorktown, 78–79
Young, Joanne, 63, 68

Picture Credits

About the Author

Michael V. Uschan has written fifteen books including *America's Founders*, a multiple biography of George Washington, Thomas Jefferson, and other leaders who helped the original thirteen colonies unite and win their independence from Great Britain, and *Westward Expansion*, which explains how Americans settled the rest of the United States. Mr. Uschan began his career as a writer and editor with United Press International, a wire service that provides stories to newspapers, radio, and television. Journalism is sometimes called "history in a hurry." Mr. Uschan considers writing history books a natural extension of skills he developed in his many years as a working journalist. He and his wife, Barbara, reside in the Milwaukee suburb of Franklin, Wisconsin.